REKINDLING THE FIRES

Val J. Peter

REKINDLING THE FIRES

An Introduction to Behavioral Spirituality

Our Sunday Visitor Publishing Division
Our Sunday Visitor, Inc.
Huntington, Indiana 46750

Copyright © 2001 by Our Sunday Visitor Publishing Division, Our Sunday Visitor, Inc.

All rights reserved. With the exception of short excerpts for critical reviews, no part of this book may be reproduced in any manner whatsoever without permission in writing from the publisher. Write:
Our Sunday Visitor Publishing Division
Our Sunday Visitor, Inc.
200 Noll Plaza
Huntington, IN 46750

ISBN: 0-87973-980-0
LCCCN: 2001-131194

Cover design by Tyler Ottinger; cover photo by John Zierten
Interior design by Sherri L. Hoffman

PRINTED IN THE UNITED STATES OF AMERICA

For my parents, brothers, and sister.

Contents

Introduction:
The Need for a New Spirituality

Hunger for the Spiritual

The dawning years of the twenty-first century might well be called "the age of spirituality." The recognition of a need for spirituality is showing up in all sorts of unexpected places: from Harvard psychiatrist Robert Coles to the coach of the Los Angeles Lakers, Phil Jackson; from Pentecostalism to the New Age; from the Branch Davidians in Waco to support groups, meditation centers, and wellness books. As the desire for spirituality grows, so too the concept of spirituality itself is undergoing enormous change.

Traditionally, spirituality was associated with a church or synagogue, with Scriptures and rituals. Not so today.

Traditionally, unchurched people were not interested in issues of faith. Not so today.

Traditionally, spirituality was part and parcel of a particular religious belief. Not so today. Today men and women who have never set foot in a church talk about finding a "spiritual path."

Clearly, there is a real spiritual hunger in our culture. But how does one find spiritual nourishment? Who knows the way?

Where Is the Gusto?

Such searching isn't limited to those without formal faith or those who have never been exposed to Christian teaching. Many Christians really and truly try to follow St. Paul's advice to "develop a new spiritual way of thinking" with little success.

I travel a great deal across America talking with people at social service agencies and with child care workers. Here I see faithful men and women and even ministers and priests whose spiritual lives are without gusto. Many have made concentrated retreats. Some know the Ignatian method of meditation. But anxiety, busyness, and tiredness seem to get in the way. In addition, public prayer or liturgy (Sunday Mass and the Divine Office) seem listless. These faithful men and women want to be reenergized. However, they don't know how to achieve it.

Let me give you an example of the kind of spiritual power so many are seeking. St. Benedict and his twin sister, St. Scholastica, were visiting together in the house at the foot of Monte Cassino. There they spent the whole day singing God's praises and conversing about the spiritual life. When Benedict wanted to leave because, according to his own monastic rule, he could not spend the night outside the monastery, Scholastica folded her hands on the table and rested her head upon them in earnest prayer. When she looked up again, there was a sudden burst of lightning and thunder accompanied by such a downpour that Benedict and his companions were unable to set foot outside the door.

"We need not be surprised that in this instance she proved mightier than her brother; she had been looking forward so long to this visit. Do we not read in St. John that God is love? Surely it is no more than right that her influence was greater than his, since hers was the greater love" (Gregory, *Dialogues*, Book II, Chapter 33).

Can We Have a Powerful Spiritual Life?

So how can we develop such a powerful spiritual life? How can you and I bring zest into our spiritual quest? How can we really encounter God?

This book is written to help you answer those questions. It uses a nontraditional approach I call "behavioral spirituality." It is my belief, based on long years of working with adults and children at Girls and Boys Town, that a Christian integration of behavioral spirituality will bring zip, zeal, and zest back into your spiritual life.

This method of rejuvenation is currently being used with success by thousands of children and families trained in Girls and Boys Town's methods. In addition (the reason why it is so dear to my heart), it is used with success by "my children," whose home life has failed at the very beginning.

Not Your Mother's Approach to Life

What makes this approach to Christian life so different?

- It starts with behavior. Behavior is something we learn through the five senses: seeing, hearing, touching, smelling, and tasting. It begins with the outside, not the inside, so it is easy to use, no matter where you are in your spiritual journey.
- It gets results right away. You can see the change immediately.
- It concentrates on skills that can be mastered by all of us . . . adults, adolescents, and children.
- It builds on revitalizing relationships.
- It avoids focusing on the disputes between liberals and conservatives in our churches today. By and large, these disputes belong to the past. They belong to the last quarter of the twentieth century. They revolve mainly around church structure and church governance and consequently they are peripheral to most people's most pressing needs.
- It makes Christianity come alive!

Spirituality is *the issue* of the twenty-first century. This little book will help you learn how to make your Christian faith be like leaven in the midst of the dough of the twenty-first century. Behavioral spirituality is one way to do this boldly.

Come, let us begin.

Chapter 1

Where We Were and Where We Are

George Santayana, the American philosopher, says, "Those who forget the past are doomed to repeat it." So before we look to the future, we need to take a look at the recent past.

At the beginning of the twentieth century, we were told that what was needed for humanity to flourish was a down-to-earth, hard-nosed, pragmatic, no-nonsense, scientific approach that would provide the world with technological wonders of every kind and a superabundance of material wealth. During most of the twentieth century, writers on Christian spirituality had to compete with three powerful forces for the attention and affection of the faithful: science and technology, humanistic psychology, and materialism masquerading as freedom.

Science and Technology

In the shining new years of the nineteenth century, spirituality and religion were roundly debunked as dead ends by such notables as Auguste Comte and Charles Darwin. Karl Marx taught that religion was the opiate of the masses and stressed that working to build a classless society would bring worldwide contentment. Sigmund Freud and his psychoanalytical followers proclaimed that religion was simply the redirection of repressed sexual impulses toward more socially acceptable goals. Finally, Nietzsche announced that God was dead.

Science was the new and exciting religion at the dawn of the twentieth century. More and more people put their hope for human betterment in the hands of those who wore lab coats. We were told repeatedly that human beings had now come of age. We were told that religion was only for children, and we were no longer children. We had outgrown our need for religion and spirituality. We were told that philosophy was only for adolescents, and we were no longer adolescents.

We were told we were mature human beings who no longer had to rely on mythical stories of the divine or on philosophical explanations. We no longer had a need for prayer, fasting, or almsgiving. In short, we no longer had a need for churches. We could now rely on the down-to-earth, no-nonsense, scientific method that would produce wondrous improvements in our own lives and in the lives of all who were privileged enough to live in these glory days.

Many Americans believed the teaching of this brave new world. They abandoned the canon of the Nicene Creed and embraced the canons of science and technology.

However, a strange thing happened when the captains of science and industry came into their own in World War I (1914-1918). Science and technology produced trench warfare, modern artillery, machine guns, land mines, fighter planes, and poison gas that killed millions and millions in their path. The people of the twentieth century were told that this was "the war to end all wars."

Then came World War II (1939-1945) with its even more destructive weapons and more horrendous loss of life, culminating in the dropping of the atom bomb on Hiroshima and

Nagasaki. The scientific advances of the day led to an Allied victory, but at what price?

Doubt in the omniscience of science began to accelerate as the Cold War and the subsequent threat of nuclear holocaust arose in the middle decades of the century; but despite the very real risk of complete annihilation, things were not simply fear-ridden. The fact is it truly was the best of times and the worst of times.

America enjoyed great economic prosperity as a result of science and technology, while at the same time and as a result of the same science and technology, the world poised on the brink of destruction.

Families never had it so good. The suburbs blossomed, shopping centers sprang up overnight. During Herbert Hoover's presidential campaign in 1928, the Republican Business Men ran an ad claiming that the Republican Party had "put the proverbial 'chicken in every pot.' And a car in every backyard, to boot." Now families had not just a chicken in every pot and a car in every garage but a TV in every living room and any number of modern appliances and other inventions that make life easier all around.

Yet, just beneath the surface, troubles were building in American family life. The divorce rate began to climb. Family dysfunction seemed to be on the rise. People felt trapped in their roles and in their suburbs. Unhappiness with unfulfilling family life began to take its toll in the 1960s as dissatisfaction with the "rat race" increased.

As the century continued, Americans questioned their blind hope for human betterment in science and technology or the goods and services spawned by them.

That's when the second shaping force of the century slipped into our collective consciousness — humanistic psychology.

Humanistic Psychology

Humanistic psychology concentrated on "getting our inner needs met." People embraced the concepts, hoping to find satisfying answers where science and technology had failed.

What did the new elixir look like?

With the rise of affluence, there came to the fore in the 1960s a group of humanistic psychologists (as distinguished from experimental psychologists and behavioral psychologists) whose views were widely promulgated.

The basic tenet began with the assumption that family life was a mess and relationships are inherently unsatisfactory. Unlike traditional Christian belief that says life itself is relational — that is, we come from the hand of the Father and return to him, and our first and primary way of defining ourselves and our needs is by our relationship with God as a child of God — the new thinking said that looking at relationships to define oneself is a dead-end and a depressing experience. The humanistic psychologist claimed people need to look inward instead of outward for identity. This process was new and interesting and led to valuable insights.

False Assumptions

But it naturally led to other assumptions.

- First, to look inward you need to define fulfillment as the process of bringing your inner needs into focus rather than the traditional view of finding fulfillment through service of others.
- Second, you have to accept the notion that a multiplicity of needs, feelings, potential, and even "selves" live within you. These inner elements (for example, parent, child, adult) can take the place of the multitude of your

relatives. Focusing on the self is decidedly easier than developing relationships with other people.

- Third, like Rousseau's noble savage, these inner elements of the self are considered to be uniformly good and happy. In Eric Berne's *Games People Play* and Thomas Harris's *I'm Okay, You're Okay*, a newborn is basically happy, fun-loving, energetic, and filled with good things. The only thing that makes the child bad or sad is the incorrect parental data that comes to the child and fills him or her with guilt, shame, and a sense of sinfulness.

From this flows the assumption that if certain feelings don't directly fulfill your inner self then they can be described as out of bounds. These may include such feelings as self-denial, mortification, shame, guilt, repentance, and fear of the Lord. Essentially, bad comes from the outside; good comes from native feelings and primal inner needs.

The result of these three assumptions was a neglect of our relationship to God as the core of our identity. In extreme cases, doing away with a relationship with God led to a denial of all sin and personal moral responsibility.

But looking to the inner self for fulfillment left a vacuum, and nature abhors a vacuum. So marketers and advertisers moved in to tell us how we could get our inner needs met. This led to the third force competing with Christian spirituality — materialism masquerading as freedom.

Materialism Masquerading as Freedom

Once the self is defined as a bundle of inner needs, it's a short step to finding the easiest way to satisfy those needs. How about a BMW, a Budweiser, a big house, perhaps a different spouse, more pleasures such as alcohol and perhaps experimenting with sex and even with drugs? Under the premise that fulfilling inner needs is the greatest good, the person with the most freedom is the one who has the least number of external restraints and who is the most empowered within to break down any internal restraints so that needs get fulfilled. The battle cry is: If it feels good, then do it (or buy it!).

This, of course, stands in glaring contrast to the traditional Christian view that the person with the greatest freedom is the most virtuous person, the person who is able to love under any circumstances, even when times are tough and there are troubles galore. A virtuous person is not an isolated individual, but a family person, a community person, and the more loving and community-oriented a person is, the more free that person is.

However, love and virtue aren't easy to sell. Advertisers began to define freedom as the ability to choose among many products and the ability to purchase and own many products and have numerous experiences. This marketing technique has been so effective that many people have come to believe they need both a wealth of material goods and a multitude of self-actualizing experiences to become fulfilled persons.

So Where Are We Now?

By the end of the last century, we had replaced external relationships with internal relationships. We replaced moderation and self-denial with economic activity guided by marketing in an expanding economy. We defined spirituality as looking inward, not outward. We were "me"-centered rather than "other"-focused.

At first, unblocking one's inner needs seemed to bring rewards. But then two things happened to derail the enthusiasm:

1. People seeking self-actualization started to grow older. As they did, sickness, accidents, and old age came along. It is

not realistic for a cancer patient to talk about self-actualization. It is very hard to find meaning in the inner search to express one's needs when one has multiple sclerosis or muscular dystrophy.

2. The search for self-fulfillment left many family relationships in shambles. Divorces increased, families broke up. Children were emotionally abandoned. It is hard to talk about self-actualization if you are in your second or third marriage and still not very happy.

On a more personal note, we at Girls and Boys Town began to experience an influx of children who no longer resembled the waifs and orphans of Father Flanagan's day. They now come with enormous problems related to drugs and alcohol, abuse of every kind, and violence and suicide. These are the children of the "me" generation. Life has failed them, not at the end or the middle, but at the beginning.

So it is not surprising that at the end of the twentieth century and the beginning of the twenty-first century, more and more Americans are seeking what St. Paul calls "a new spiritual way of thinking." A belief in a Higher Power is now, at the beginning of the twenty-first century, embraced with the same enthusiasm with which it was rejected a hundred years ago.

But, of course, there is a difference. Many New Agers today reject traditional Christianity in its historical unfolding. Some replace it not just with crystals and séances but with a myriad of self-help groups ranging from cancer groups to survivor groups of various kinds of abuse, from Jungian psychology with a goddess motif to Eastern mysticism.

In addition to these New Agers, many Christians of every denomination are experiencing a deep spiritual hunger based on the realization that humans "do not live on bread alone."

The bread of science, the bread of technology, the bread of neo-conservatism, the bread of Enneagrams, of Meyers-Briggs tests, of Abraham Maslow's self-actualization, or Erik Erikson's life stages — all of these fail to satisfy. Men and women are looking for a more appropriate spirituality for the twenty-first century, a spirituality marked with consistency between what they practice and what they believe.

What We Really Need

What do people really need spiritually? Some answers may be found in George Gallup, Jr.'s report on the American people's *Six Basic Spiritual Needs in the 1990s.*

1. "The need to believe that life is meaningful and has a purpose." Gallup's studies show that seventy percent of Americans say that this is a very important issue. And at the same time, sixty-six percent of the people interviewed said that "most churches and synagogues today are not effective in helping people find meaning in life." The New Age movement is, in my opinion, a symptom of this phenomenon.

2. "The need for a sense of community and deeper relationships." With the increased emphasis on individualism of the past decades, with the increased pace of life, with the increasing instances of meeting others on the freeway and in long lines at the supermarket, this sense of individualism becomes a kind of loneliness.

3. "The need to be appreciated and respected." Gallup found, not surprisingly, that the more people feel close to God, the better they feel about themselves. The more consistency there is between faith and practice, the happier they are. So thinking, feeling, and behavior really do go together.

4. "The need to be listened to — to be heard." This is a call for a bottom-up approach rather more than just a top-down approach. People need to know that their views are taken seriously.

5. "The need to feel that one is growing in faith." People don't like spiritual mediocrity. I have heard from an increasing number of people comments such as: "I did something the other day which I know is wrong and yet I don't feel bad about it and that bothers me a lot." People want, and need, to believe they are developing in their relationship with God.

6. "The need for practical help in developing a mature faith." People clearly need help in learning how to grow in faith, how to develop an adult faith, and how to overcome the inconsistency between what they believe and what they do.

So where do we start?

That's where behavioral spirituality fits in.

SUMMARY Despite the idea that science and technology could cure all of humanity's ills, we continue to experience a profound hunger for the spiritual life. How to develop a spiritual way of living that is effective in today's world is one of the major challenges of the twenty-first century.

Chapter 2

A New Model for a New People

Exactly what are we talking about? What is behavioral spirituality and what does it mean in our everyday lives?

It's simple. Behavioral spirituality says that what we do affects what we think and what we feel. If we change the way we act, we will naturally change the way we think and feel.

Let's take a mundane example. You decide you want to get healthy, so you begin to improve your diet, join a gym, and start regular workouts. Gradually, as you continue to lift your weights and eat your veggies, you begin to think of yourself not as a couch potato but as someone who works out and eats right. As you see the changes in your body, you begin to feel better about yourself and the way you look.

The same is true on a spiritual level. You decide you want to improve your relationship with God, so you begin to act more charitably, read more Scripture, participate more fully at Mass. Gradually, as you perform works of charity and spend more time in prayer, you will begin to become less judgmental and more compassionate, less materialistic and more generous. In short, you change the way you think and feel because you change your behavior.

Behavior, thoughts, and feelings are three legs on the stool of your life. If any one of the three is broken or missing, you are going to end up on the floor. However, one of them is easier to focus on than the others — behavior. It's a lot easier to change what you do than it is to change the way you think or the way you feel.

That's precisely what behavioral spirituality is all about. It's a way to get all three legs of your stool in good order by working first on the leg that will produce the quickest and most dramatic results. Once all three legs are in good working order, then you can sometimes change the way you act by changing your feelings or your thinking, but why make it harder on yourself than need be? You can legitimately take the easy way out!

In the next chapters, let's look at how this all works together to create a new way of spiritual life.

SUMMARY   Behavior, thoughts, and feelings are intimately related. When we alter one, we naturally change the others. Behavioral spirituality uses this natural law to create positive changes.

Chapter 3

It All Starts with Behavior

We need to start our quest for a new spirituality, not with thoughts, not with feelings, but with behavior.

Why behavior? Why not start with thoughts and feelings? Let's look at some of the reasons:

- Developing spirituality through behavior is a practical place to start because it is easier to gain mastery of behavior than thinking or feelings.
- Starting with behavior takes less time to show results.
- Starting with behavior allows one to develop more strategies and motives and provides more feedback.
- Starting with behavior follows the developmental process.
- Beginning with behavior gives you measurable and outcome-based results.

In other words, we start with behavior because that's where we are most likely to see immediate, measurable results. After all, if you are allergic to shellfish, you can try to deal with your allergy by not thinking about shellfish or by having positive feelings about shellfish or you can begin by not eating shellfish. If you have a serious or life-threatening allergy, you can have all the positive feelings or thoughts you want about shellfish, but your thoughts and feelings aren't going to help you if you gobble down a serving of crab cakes and go into anaphylactic shock.

The Key to Change

For those who want to develop a mature Christian faith and overcome the inconsistency between what we believe and feel and what we do, behavioral spirituality is the key. There are several reasons why this is true:

- *It's easy to determine right from wrong behavior.* We all make judgments about ourselves and others first and foremost on behavior. The old adage is true — actions do speak louder than words.
- *Scripture stresses the importance of behavior.* Take the Last Judgment, for instance. It is described foremost in terms of behavior: feeding the hungry, giving drink to the thirsty, clothing the naked (see Matthew 25:31-46). Alternatively, look at the Good Samaritan. He didn't just sit around having good thoughts and warm empathetic feelings (see Luke 10:29-37). He did something worthwhile.
- *Jesus himself says behavior is essential to eternal life.* We are told to come and follow the Lord, not just have positive thoughts and favorable feelings toward him (see Mark 10:17). We are told to take up our cross, not just think about it (see Mark 8:34). We are told to act, not just think.

So What's It All About?

I hope that you are willing to accept the idea that the way to enliven your spiritual life is by doing something. Let's now look at some of the basic concepts underlying changing behavior to create a new spirituality.

1. Spiritual health is interconnected with your entire life.

You can't make changes in your spiritual life without making changes in your entire life. The holistic approach has a noble lineage all the way back to Aristotle, who taught that there is a substantial (not accidental) union between the soul and the body in human beings. Current developments in the neurosciences underline this. Just look at the interface between immunology, neurology, and endocrinology.

The interconnected nature of spiritual health was hinted at in the ancient adage *"Mens sana in corpore sano"* ("A healthy mind in a healthy body").

Spiritual health in America today is the interface of physical (exercise, eating healthy foods, managing stress), the social/emotional (building friendships, giving service, listening empathetically, creating energy), the mental (reading, visualizing, planning, writing, developing talents, learning new skills), and the spiritual (meditating, praying, practicing the corporal and spiritual works of mercy, reading the Scriptures, reconnecting to following the Lord). You have to have all of these in order to be truly spiritually healthy.

2. The past has lessons for the present.

This approach integrates the wisdom of the Christian past with new behavioral insights from our own day. This holistic approach shows that the past is as important as the present or the future; that those who went before us were not lacking in wisdom or insight and grace, and that in their love of God and neighbor, they carry with them a kind of role modeling vitally needed today.

3. Changing behavior over time can change those emotions that hamper our spiritual growth.

Often problems for those interested in developing spiritually occur with emotions. David Goleman in *Emotional Intelligence* (1995) argues persuasively that the development and mastery of emotions is just as important as the development and mastery of the intellect.

Here is where the concept of the "empty self" comes into play. The "empty self" is a term used frequently to describe the person who has to use consumer spending and vicarious experiences to fill what is otherwise an emotional vacuum.

The children who come to Girls and Boys Town are a good example. Many of them have been abandoned by the man who fathered them; a man who was a stranger, showing up sporadically or not at all. Their mothers are often hooked on drugs and alcohol and are thus disabled from being real mothers. These children do not feel loved or cared for or worthwhile. They do not have conversation skills or relationship skills. They have little or no religious tradition and no impulse control. Superficial, temporary liaisons are seen as precious because that is all they have experienced. They engage in acquiring and consuming goods and services, legal and illegal. They are "empty selves."

But they aren't the only ones. Think of all the children who are in otherwise "good families," who have their own rooms, their own TV's, their own phones, their own VCR's, their own Game Boys — and who are very lonely. They have little ability to express emotions except through outbursts of anger. They have poor communication skills and meager success with peer relations. Their self is constructed of brand-name clothes, seeing the right movies, and listening to the "correct" music. The self is tragically empty here too.

It is impossible to experience true spiritual growth without first untangling faulty emotions through wholesome and right relationships.

4. Doing is intimately linked with thinking and feeling.

The fact is that if one engages in a specific behavior for a sufficient period of time, there will usually be a corresponding change in one's thinking and one's feelings.

One of the boys at Girls and Boys Town gave a clear example of this. He was only with us for a week when he ran away and was caught shoplifting. I picked him up from the police station, and on the way home, he said, "What do I have to do first?" I told him the first thing he had to do was to apologize and say he was sorry to the family he was living with. His response was: "I'm not going to do that. I know your trick. If I start saying I'm sorry, I'm going to start to feel sorry."

Yep, that's how it works. When we change our actions, over time we change our thoughts as well. That is we why say "a good act of contrition" in the Sacrament of Reconciliation. If you start saying you are sorry, you may start to feel sorry.

5. Thoughts, feelings, and behavior are interactive.

Let's take a common example. Christmas is coming. You think to yourself: "We have to stop and visit our in-laws and that is going to be another disaster just like last year." This negative *thinking* turns into negative *feelings* of aversion, sadness, anger, and mild depression. Then this combination of negative thoughts and negative feelings leads to negative *behavior* during the visit which, in turn, reinforces the negative thoughts and the negative feelings, which then lead to creating negative behavior. And on and on around the legs of the stool.

On the other hand, positive behavior will create positive thoughts and feelings, which, in turn, will generate more positive behavior. For instance, instead of thinking about how awful Christmas with the in-laws is going to be, try a different approach. "I know last year at Christmas, visiting the in-laws was very negative (*behavior*). However, I have some *thoughts* on how to make it successful this year. Those thoughts make me *feel* more hopeful and positive about the visit."

If you begin to think that the visit will be better, you will begin to feel more positive about it and subsequently you will begin to act in ways that will make the visit more pleasant.

The unfortunate fact is we live in an age that not only celebrates feelings, but grants them a kind of infallibility. So often we feel like doing something and immediately do it, only afterwards trying to think up reasons that justify it. Let's call this what it is: plain, old rationalization.

It shouldn't be surprising that many people today automatically believe that what they feel has just got to be true. For example, if you feel ugly, you must be ugly. If you feel like you are "no good," you must be "no good." If you feel sexy, you must be sexy. Unexamined feelings are accepted on face value.

Looking at this belief more objectively, we realize our feelings can either tell us the truth or they can lie to us. So also our thoughts can lie to us or can tell us the truth. However, our behavior can seldom deceive us. Consider for a moment a person who is stopped for drunk driving. He or she might not feel drunk. The person may, in fact, feel completely sober. However, his weaving over the white line proves that he is, in fact, intoxicated no matter what he may think or feel.

Because of our tendency to deceive ourselves, we must learn how to create the proper balance of feelings and thoughts with action in order to become creative, energetic, and enthusiastic individuals.

Before we take a closer look at how this works in the spiritual life, let's talk about some of the soul-threatening problems of distorted thinking and warped feelings that prevent us from energizing our spiritual lives.

SUMMARY The ancient maxim *"Orthopraxis* helps develop *orthodoxis"* (that is, "Right action develops right thinking") is the key to lasting change. Change your behavior and you automatically change your thoughts and your feelings.

Chapter 4

What You Think Does Count

The emphasis on behavior doesn't mean that thoughts and feelings are unimportant. They are the other two legs of the stool of Christian life. True, right behavior develops right thinking, and right thinking helps us determine appropriate feelings, but distorted thinking leads to distorted feelings that then lead to distorted behavior.

Because so much of our culture relies on distorted thinking and feelings, we need to be able to recognize them so that we can detect the changes created by our new behaviors.

I Can See Clearly Now

Sometimes our distorted thinking is so ingrained and so habitual, it's hard to recognize it until someone points it out. This distorted thinking naturally leads to negative feelings and negative behaviors — with obviously negative results.

Let's take this example. You are scheduled to go over to your in-laws for dinner. You say to yourself: "These people have never liked me." (There is quite a bit of evidence for that.) "They are selfish and totally insensitive." (That's an exaggeration, but there is evidence for their selfishness and insensitivity.) "It's going to be a disastrous evening." (This statement is a self-fulfilling prophecy.)

If you dwell on these thoughts long enough, they will trigger feelings of bitterness, anger, dislike, contempt, frustration, and hopelessness. By the time you get to your in-laws, you are acting aloof, rude, arrogant, and haughty. In other words, negative thinking leads to negative feelings and that leads to negative behavior.

Instead of starting with negative thoughts, you could have said to yourself: "Yes, I know we have to go to our in-laws next Thursday, and it has often been a negative experience. But I believe if I work on picking out positive things, it can be a positive experience." In other words, don't plan to lament your fate, but rather plan to make it a positive event insofar as you can. These positive thoughts tend to trigger positive feelings and you become more comfortable, more confident, and more hopeful. Then, no matter how the evening turns out, you can say to yourself, "I am proud of myself and I helped make my spouse and kids happy too."

Please Take This Personally

One kind of distorted thinking is ugly propaganda, pure and simple, and it almost always triggers a behavioral response based not on fact, but on emotion.

One chilling example comes to mind from the past century.

Adolph Hitler communicated to his followers a profound sense that Germany was "going to hell in a handbasket" because of the Jews: their policies, their practices, and their personages. So strong was this "brainwashing" that as soon as one of his followers saw a Jew, in person or in print, negative feelings arose immediately: contempt, disgust, despair, exasperation, frustration, and pessimism. The death camps of the Nazi regime were the logical behavioral outgrowth of such distorted thinking. In a vicious circle, wholesale slaughter of the

Jews reinforced the "rightness" of anti-Semitic feelings that, in turn, supported the "correctness" of anti-Semitic thinking that sustained the "necessity" for anti-Semitic death camps.

A more recent example occurred during the presidential election of 2000. Here they were called spin doctors. The country was almost evenly divided among those who believed the election of George W. Bush was a harbinger of societal disaster and those who were certain that the election of Al Gore spelled complete ruin for the country. The sight of protestors very nearly coming to blows over such distorted thinking is one of the sadder sights of the beginning of the new millennium.

There are many other examples that strike closer to home. In our own churches, one has to look no further than the extremists of the left and the right for whom the sight of certain "enemies" (church leaders or theologians) creates emotional outbursts out of all proportion to reality.

Those Madison Avenue Blues

The biggest creator of distorted thinking has to be the marketing industry. It is based almost entirely on clever imaging that plays on our insecurities. In turn, our insecurities cause us to use what is called "emotional reasoning," a kind of distorted thinking that runs a mental tape which says: "My feelings are most important. I shouldn't neglect them. I should especially trust my negative feelings. I have no need to ask whether my negative feelings are appropriate or not. I should just trust them. I can't control them anyway."

Madison Avenue uses our faulty thinking to turn our attention to our feelings, knowing that will, in turn, impact our behavior. Again, the three legs of the stool come into play — often to our detriment.

Stop in the Name of Thought?

Obviously the answer isn't to stop thinking. If we didn't use the brains God gave us, rather than being little less than the angels, we would be little less than the beasts! No, we need to think, but we also need to think the correct thoughts.

How do we do that? First by being aware of what we are thinking. Once we start to pay attention to the thoughts that constantly bombard us, we can begin to see where we are being misled and where we are going astray. But even more important, we need to change our behavior so that our thoughts will naturally become more balanced.

However, before we do that, we still need to consider those ever-elusive feelings.

SUMMARY Thoughts are important because distorted thinking leads to distorted behavior. We need to sort out our thinking so that we can begin to see how changes in behavior really do create changes in our thought patterns.

Chapter 5

Feelings Matter

The link between what we feel and what we believe is both intense and fraught with danger. It is so easy for us to get caught in the trap of accepting our feelings as reflective of reality.

For instance:

- If feel ugly, I must be ugly.
- If I feel powerless, I must be powerless.
- If I feel depressed, it must mean that my life is pointless.
- If I feel angry, that means somebody must have taken advantage of me.
- If I feel stupid, it must mean I am stupid.
- If I feel you don't love me or understand me, then you must not love or understand me.

This is distorted thinking. Let me give you a real-life example. I know a lot of girls who feel they are unattractive and even ugly. They believe that feelings don't lie and can always be trusted, so they say to themselves: "I feel ugly so I must be ugly." Then, in turn, they begin to act as if they were ugly, devaluing themselves and sometimes even doing things that are downright harmful because they began with the focus on their unreliable feelings. They don't realize that the marketing surrounding their lives puts feelings in their hearts and thoughts in their heads that say: "If you don't look like a model on the most recent cover of *Seventeen*, you are ugly."

The reality may be quite different. After all, it has been shown time and time again that almost no girl (except for a few brief moments in a photo session) looks like a model for any period of time. (And even pictures of most models are airbrushed before publication to be even more perfect.)

Emotional Reasoning

Mental-health professionals call this reliance on feelings to direct thoughts and behavior "emotional reasoning." Adolescents are very likely to suffer from such emotional reasoning, but they aren't the only ones. How many ministers and priests were told in the seminary they would never be "good preachers"? Those thoughts triggered feelings of being inadequate, ignorant, incompetent, inferior, and indecisive. They hated the thought of preaching and thus neglected preparation. They felt inadequate going into the pulpit and their sermons were terrible.

How many moms and dads do you know who were told they would never "amount to anything"? They got through their schooling by doing what they were told. As with those unfortunate ministers and priests who were told they would never be good preachers, these moms and dads were bombarded with negative thoughts that triggered feelings of being inadequate, ignorant, and so forth. And those feelings are still with them. No wonder their behavior corresponds with those thoughts and feelings. No wonder they aren't good parents. No wonder they don't take their responsibilities seriously. No wonder they do what pop psychology tells them to do. They act about as inadequate and inferior as others have come to expect. And because their behavior isn't much, not much is expected of them.

Ironically, senior citizens can still be vulnerable to such emotional reasoning. A whole generation of seniors has been convinced to "hoard your money. You won't be able to trust your kids. They won't take care of you." Those negative feelings of fear, abandonment, and neglect trigger negative thoughts and subsequent negative behaviors. It's little wonder seniors in our day seem much, much more selfish, self-centered, whining, and complaining than in past generations.

If It Feels Good . . .

In fact, much of our entire culture is predicated on emotional reasoning. How many times have you heard some variation on the theme — if it feels good, do it? Many of society's ills, from rampant divorce to teenage pregnancies to an epidemic of drug use, can be traced back to overreliance on feelings as a guide to a happy life. The right to pursue happiness granted in the Declaration of Independence has become a right to feel good, no matter what the consequences. We have become so reliant on our feelings that we use them to justify egregious and often outrageous behavior. And then we wonder why we are so spiritually and morally bankrupt.

There Is an Easy Answer!

So what's the answer? I'm sure you've guessed. It starts with changing behavior. What the adolescent, the priest, the parent, the grandparent need to do is to start acting like heroes. They have to start engaging in positive behavior regardless of their negative thoughts and feelings.

Why? Because heroes do that all the time. The message is clear: "If you act like a hero long enough, your feelings and thoughts will change from negative to positive." As the saying goes, "Practice makes perfect." One of the great paradoxes is that even if you begin by practicing, you are guaranteed to end by doing better, thinking better, and feeling better.

Now, let's see how this all impacts our spiritual lives.

SUMMARY Feelings are important, but in our culture feelings have become paramount — if it feels good, do it! We have become so reliant on our feelings that we use them to justify egregious and often outrageous behavior. And then we wonder why we are so spiritually and morally bankrupt.

Chapter 6

I'm from Missouri, Show Me!

We've looked at how thoughts, feelings, and behavior interact in the abstract, but let's see how they play out in real life.

I FEEL, Therefore I Am Right

Toby Smith is thirty-five years old. When he was a boy, his mom and dad tried to make sure he felt good about himself. Whenever Toby made a mistake, one of them was right there to tell him it wasn't his fault or skim over his error. He grew up thinking he was someone special because his parents never raised their voices or took things away from him when he misbehaved. He quickly learned he could pretty much do whatever he wanted because his parents would bend over backwards to make sure he never felt bad or unhappy. The Smiths went so far as to argue with teachers and the principal at his school when he got bad grades or broke the rules. They said that punishing Toby would damage his self-esteem. His parents were simultaneously overly permissive and overly protective. He didn't need to do his own thinking, so the ability to discern atrophied. His feelings began to control his life. There was no balance between thinking, feeling, and behavior.

He was successful in life for a variety of reasons, mostly because his mom and dad set him up in business and helped him out whenever he got in trouble. He married a woman who mothered him and reinforced his parents' idealization of him.

For Toby, feelings are all-important. Toby is a spoiled brat because there is no balance in his life. For him to be happy, he needs to get his way. He is stuck in self-absorption, yet a spiritual ache resides within. Toby knows something isn't right. He wonders if someone — maybe his parents or his wife — has damaged his self-esteem. He is bored with his life and has no interest in God.

All That Matters Is What I THINK

Let's look at another example. When Jennifer was ten, her mom started to have long talks with her about being able to think for herself. Her mom told her how important it was to assess a situation, consider the facts, and make a responsible decision. Her mom reasoned that by teaching Jennifer to rely on her thinking skills, she could make the right choices as she grew up.

These discussions continued through grade school, junior high, and high school. By the time Jennifer was in her teens, she learned to look at situations from many different angles and come up with options about how to respond or behave.

That was all well and good, except that Jennifer's mom didn't teach her much about appropriate feelings and behaviors. Appropriate feelings for Jennifer might have included some sensitivity to others, learning how to feel the hurt, frustration, and anxiety of others. However, a terrible imbalance was created. Jennifer never learned to accept input from others. She didn't know how to give and take. She only knew how to think about situations and make her own decisions. If someone disagreed, too bad. Her way was the only way.

Jennifer is stuck in the developmental stage of late childhood and adolescence where independent thoughts and feelings are dominant. She is a snob living in splendid isolation. She cannot commit herself to anything but her own ideas.

Jennifer has applied the same approach to religion and spirituality. She has moved from one church to another looking for that elusive something missing in her life. She is a prime candidate for a cult — another instance of imbalance.

But I'm DOING It Right!

Finally, let's look at Father Mike Murphy, whose dad believed in obedience, respect, and "getting things done the right way." When the alarm rang at 6:30, Murphy and his two brothers jumped out of bed, got dressed, made their beds, and dashed for the breakfast table. Following the family's strict rules was mandatory for the Murphy kids. The consequences were simple: do what you are supposed to and you stay out of trouble. Mess up and you spend painful time on a work detail. There was little time for hugging or other mushy displays of affection. Forget feelings. What is needed is right behavior.

Father Murphy's dad made it clear that he would do the thinking for the family. As the years went by, Mr. Murphy took pride in the fact that his kids — including Mike — were the best behaved in school and could be counted on to do what they were told to do without back talk or questions. It didn't matter much to him that the kids didn't have many friends or that they rarely told him that they loved him. Disciplined behavior was the key to success. And his kids were going to be successful.

Mike saw his love of God in terms of behavior as well. He loved God. His behavior as a child and in the seminary showed it. He also believed God and the Church were responsible for doing all his thinking. He transferred his unquestioning patterns from his father to God and the Church.

Now he says that he doesn't "get as much out of the priest-hood as I would like to."

Father Mike Murphy trusted his dad and stifled his own thoughts and feelings. His love of God was one-dimensional: right behavior is all that matters. His life was unbalanced and thus was destined to be unsettling and unfulfilling over the long haul. He is a prime candidate for having a secret romance.

So What's the Answer?

The remedy to all three of these sad situations is changed behavior. If this still doesn't make sense, think about this for a minute. Let's say you trust a used-car dealer and so you invest in a car he tells you is "in good working order and will give you years and years of service." Then in two weeks it is apparent that fifteen hundred dollars' worth of work has to be done immediately just to keep the vehicle running.

Well, what's the remedy for your mistaken trust in the used-car salesman? Never buy a used car again? Of course not. Rather it is: "I'll be more cautious the next time I go to a car dealer." In other words, I will develop better controls over believing and trusting.

The remedy to a broken heart is not to stop loving. It is to learn how to love and to receive love. In the same way, the remedy for improper beliefs and thoughts is not to stop think-ing or believing, but rather to learn behaviors that can change the faulty patterns.

Now let's see how that might work in the lives of Toby, Jennifer, and Father Murphy.

Toby is a good example of someone who, if he really wants to change, needs to start by changing his behavior. Let me repeat: he doesn't need to start by changing his thoughts and feelings. He needs to start by *changing his behavior*. He needs to engage in behavior that is other-centered rather than focused entirely on himself and his feelings.

He could begin with giving money to charity, helping those less fortunate, going to church, and being more understanding with his kids. The point is that there is plenty to do – he just has to begin doing it. After a while he will find himself *thinking new thoughts* by listening to the Gospel in a new non-self-absorbed way. The fact is, the best way for Toby to achieve the balance he wants and ease the ache in his soul is to change his behavior and then let his feelings and thoughts follow.

Jennifer could start gaining perspective by joining a faith community with a good spiritual director who can help her learn balance between thinking, feeling, and behavior. In the meantime she needs to develop some behaviors that are other-centered: listening, counseling, teaching someone else, trying to understand others' opinions, and trying to work with others' ideas. In other words, she needs to start behaving in ways that can help her experience feelings of empathy and compassion. Once she has experienced some of those feelings through changed behavior, her thought patterns can change as well.

The first thing that Father Murphy could do would be to start working with a group of other priests who are as behaviorally faithful to the Church as he is and who, on the other hand, think for themselves; priests who can recognize and accept their feelings and can talk openly about them. In the process, Father Murphy's feelings about the priesthood are likely to change in a positive way.

Making changes in behavior is the only sure way to create a new way of thinking and feeling. So where's the best place to begin making changes in our spiritual lives?

SUMMARY Some people get trapped in incorrect feelings, some in incorrect thinking, and some in incorrect behavior. The solution to all three life-draining situations is the same — correct behavior.

Chapter 7

'Teach Us How to Pray'

Prayer, almsgiving, and fasting are skills, a series of day-to-day steps within a matrix that all of us can use in our everyday lives to change our behavior and consequently change our thinking and our feelings. A good place to begin is with prayer.

Just the Facts

The first thing to do is to figure out some facts about prayer:

- Prayer is not emptying your head of all thought.
- Prayer is not the same as thinking.
- Prayer tends to stop what is going on in your mind, your heart, and your innermost being.
- Prayer involves physical relaxation and reduction of anxiety.
- Prayer takes preparation.
- Prayer involves morphological changes. In other words, you change your bodily position. Each culture has bodily positions such as kneeling, standing, lying prostrate. Most of them work just fine.
- Prayer requires a quiet place – the more sacred, the better.
- Prayer involves lifting your mind and heart to God.
- Christian prayer is focused on the Three Persons in one God and not on a state of consciousness. Other types of

prayer, such as Hindu meditation, are centered on seeking a higher stage of consciousness.

- Christian prayer is a grace from God. God gives us the gift of prayer. "We do not even know how to pray as we ought, but the Spirit himself intercedes for us with sighs too deep for words" (Romans 8:26).

The goal of prayer is to open our minds and hearts to the presence of the Lord, letting him into our lives. Developing this interpersonal relationship is very much like tuning a radio in to the right station. You have to know what wavelength the station is on. When you pray, you have to find God's wavelength.

Begin to ACT

Prayer can be either formal (using someone else's words and making them your own in a public or private setting) or informal (using your own words.)

One of the best ways to begin informal prayer is by using ACTS:

A *Is for Adoration*
This means to give praise to God: "I adore."

C *Is for Confession*
This means to tell your sins to God: "I confess."

T *Is for Thanksgiving*
This means to be grateful to God: "I am thankful."

S *Is for Supplication*
This means to request something from God: "I ask."

Tips on Praying Privately

The Twelve Apostles asked the Lord, "Teach us how to pray." They had the privilege of being with the Lord himself on this earth. Is it any wonder, then, that we have trouble figuring out how to pray?

One night I was saying my prayers near the altar in Girls and Boys Town's Dowd Chapel. I heard a boy come in and start to weep in the back. He finally came forward, and when I asked him what was wrong, he said: "Father, would you teach me how to pray? Nobody has ever taught me. I don't know how."

I said: *"This is the first lesson . . . you have to sit here and be totally quiet and put yourself in the presence of the Lord, opening your heart to him and letting him love you."*

I went back to my praying, and in about five minutes, I heard him crying again. When I asked him what was wrong, he said: "Shush, Father, I'm just letting the Lord love me."

Letting the Lord love you: that's the first guide to life-enriching prayer. In order to do that, place yourself in the presence of the Lord in a holy place, perhaps in a church before the tabernacle for focus. Next, like the boy who talked with me, open your heart to the Lord's love. Let the Lord's love touch you, envelop you, delight you.

If you struggle, remember that love is not an instinct, but rather a learned behavior, and you can't love unless you have first been loved. Therefore, letting the Lord love you is essential if you wish to know how to pray.

The second guideline is simple: avoid gimmicks.

There is a superstitious belief afoot in the New Age spirituality that says a religious experience is like a high, like an al-

tered state of consciousness. Therefore, for New Age followers, prayer can (and should) involve substances that bring them
to a higher state such as drugs and alcohol. In addition, certain objects, according to New Agers, are more powerful ways
to enhance your prayers. If you use the right crystal or talis-
man, your prayers are sure to be answered.

All of that is patently false. Letting the Lord love you is a
religious experience, even if you don't feel "high." If you let
this experience form your spiritual life, remarkable results will
ensue.

*The third guideline answers the question "What should we
use to pray with?" The simplest answer is "Whatever is available."* Remember the story of St. Ignatius of Loyola? He was a
professional soldier whose hip was broken by a cannonball
when he was fighting a battle near Pamplona, Spain. While he
was recuperating, the only books available to him were *The
Life of Christ* and *The Lives of the Saints*. He started with what
was available and moved on from there.

As you begin to pray, start with something you have always
wanted to read and felt you should, perhaps one of the four Gospels or St. Paul's Letter to the Romans. If you want some addi-
tional insights, use a good commentary such as William Barclay's,
which is readily available. Of course it has a few spots in it that
aren't in accord with Catholic teaching, but most of us are mature
enough to handle that. It's good reading. And good behavior!

Praying in the Midst of Many

Private prayer is important to Christian life, but public
prayer is equally important. We are fortunate as Catholic Christians to have two great public prayers — the Eucharist and the

Divine Office. If you let these formal prayers take root in your spiritual life, remarkable results will ensue here too.

It is here, in the public prayer of the Church, that we can easily see the relationship between behavior, thinking, and feeling.

Behavior

How many times have you seen people come to Mass with the same attitude they would have going to a restaurant: loud, unfocused, irreverent. Is it little wonder they say they don't get anything out of Church?

When you come to Mass, your behavior has to be one of reverence, awe, and openness. You must be ready to encounter the divine.

Thinking

If you are behaving in an appropriate manner, right thinking will follow. You will begin to realize that "the Lord will slowly form us into his Body as a community if we are both hearers of the Word (Liturgy of the Word) and doers of the Word (Liturgy of the Eucharist)." A phrase that was popularized in the liturgical movement fifty years ago is still true today: "We need to pray the Mass, not just at the Mass."

Feelings

If your behavior is correct, your thinking will follow and your feelings will fall into place. Let them. Let positive feelings that come from being in a holy place touch you, overwhelm you, and fill you. The ancient gargoyles hanging on the great cathedrals of Europe symbolize chasing out negative feelings as one entered the great and sacred space. Even without gargoyles to remind us, we need to lay aside feelings of frustration, anger, alienation, and impatience and instead let flow into us the feelings of sacredness, awe, majesty, faith, hope, and love.

Just Do It

The wonderful thing about prayer is that there isn't a right or a wrong way to pray. God isn't keeping a report card and giving us grades on how well we "do" our prayers. Prayer is ultimately a conversation, a relationship with the One who loves us. There are as many different ways to pray as there are people praying them.

If you love to sing, sing. It is said that those who sing pray twice, so you may be getting a double bonus.

If you love to dance, dance. David danced for joy before the Ark of the Covenant.

If you love to write, write. We would not have some of the great prayers of the saints if they hadn't put their thoughts on paper.

If you love to paint, paint. Blessed Fra Angelico, the Dominican artist, used his talent to create lasting images of prayer.

Nike was on to something when the company adopted "Just do it" as its motto. In prayer, as in life, it doesn't so much matter what you do as the fact that you do it.

Pray something.

Pray some way.

Pray today.

SUMMARY   Prayer is one of the three time-honored techniques for combating apathy in the spiritual life.

Chapter 8

Give and It Shall Be Given Unto You

Almsgiving

Almsgiving is more than just writing a check for a charity in order to get a tax deduction. True almsgiving is a radical act of faith made concrete. Christ pointed this out in the story of the widow's mite. Although a wealthy man gave large sums from his abundance, Jesus said that the widow who gave a penny from her poverty was the one who was to be blessed. In order for almsgiving to make a difference it has to hurt — no pain, no gain.

Almsgiving is difficult in an age of credit cards and marketing. No matter how much money people make, most of us are "dead broke." Yet, if we are to conquer apathy, we must take seriously Christ's admonition to give as the widow who put in her mite.

Begin at the Beginning

There are three places to start with almsgiving. The first is financial, literally giving from your financial resources. While tithing — that is, giving ten percent of your income to the church and other charities — is an admirable goal, few of us can make that leap of faith immediately. However, most of us give far less than we could — or should. The best way to begin giving is to *begin* giving. Commit yourself to giving a certain amount each week that stretches your comfort zone. If you are stuck in a routine of giving five dollars every Sunday, try doubling or tripling it. Give just a little more than you think you can; that's what true almsgiving is all about. Remember, it's not supposed to be easy!

In order to begin giving even a little more than you have been accustomed, you may have to make some changes in your lifestyle. Figure out what goods and services you will cease purchasing in order to give. Before you begin to panic, remember you don't have to sell your house and donate the entire proceeds. Instead, give up that daily *caffè latte* or stop buying books and use the library and give the money you would have spent. Bypass a treat and donate that money. Eat a simple meal once a week and give the money you saved. And if you are already giving, give a little more. Remember, God will never be outgiven and the measure with which you give is the measure with which it will be given back to you!

More Than Money

The second facet of almsgiving involves the corporal works of mercy. These physical actions aren't always discussed in today's society because we all too often leave them up to social service agencies. However, these traditional actions require both sacrifices of time and money and are an excellent way to combat spiritual apathy.

In fact, in our modern world, giving up our time is sometimes more difficult than merely writing a check to a charity because it involves down-and-dirty, hands-on action. While it's not necessary to do all of these, find a couple that appeal to you and your situation and do what you can do.

One thing to remember — Mother Teresa of Calcutta said that our society was among the most impoverished on the face of the earth because of our loneliness and isolation. Therefore, it isn't always necessary to go out on the streets looking for someone to help. The wealthy doctor down the street may be in as much need of an act of mercy as the drug addict holding up a sign asking for money on the corner. Look for the opportunities to perform works of mercy in the areas where God has placed you.

Here are a few suggestions. I'm sure you can think of many more.

1. Feeding the hungry.

- Work at a soup kitchen.
- Start an emergency food pantry at your church or contribute to one that already exists.
- Invite a lonely neighbor in for a meal.
- Give a fast-food restaurant coupon to a homeless person.
- Take a meal to a new mom or an invalid.

2. Sheltering the homeless.

- Travel to a Third World country to help literally build a house.
- Take in an unwed mother during her pregnancy.
- Work with your city to provide low-cost housing.
- Pay the rent for someone who is unemployed.

3. Giving drink to the thirsty.

- Buy a soft drink and give it to a traffic cop on a hot day.
- Take bottled water to a shut-in.

- Have a cup of coffee with a lonely acquaintance.
- Make sure your community's drinking water is safe.
- Provide a glass of lemonade to the person cutting your grass.

4. Clothing the naked.

- Clean your closet and give things you don't wear to charity.
- Contribute to a giving tree at Christmas.
- Ask your local school if there is a poor child who needs a winter coat and provide one.
- Donate outgrown baby items to a pregnancy support program.

5. Visiting the sick.

- This one is easy. We all know someone who has cancer or another terminal illness, but we can also just visit those who are down with the flu or under the weather with a common cold.

6. Visiting the imprisoned.

- Volunteer at the local jail.
- Teach reading at a youth detention center.
- Go to a nursing or rest home.
- Drop by the home of a new mom who can't get out.
- Visit an elderly friend or relative.

7. Burying the dead.

- During the days of the plague, burying the dead was much more literal than it is today, but it still is an act of mercy to attend a funeral and help the grieving.

Eye Toward Heaven

The third aspect of almsgiving centers on the spiritual works of mercy. It's unlikely you've ever heard a sermon about these actions, but that doesn't mean they are important. In fact, the spiritual works of mercy are particularly hard for us moderns to do because they involve not merely a sacrifice of time or money but a personal commitment to another person. In a very real sense, they require one to take the place of Christ. So, to round out your almsgiving, pick one of the spiritual works and make the sacrifice.

1. Instructing the ignorant.

- This can mean something as formal as teaching an inquiry class for new converts, but it can also mean telling people about your own faith over a cup of tea and a muffin. How about mentoring?

2. Advising the doubtful.

- We all know people who question the existence of God or the truth of Christianity. This act of mercy calls us to share our own experiences in order to build faith in others.

3. Consoling the depressed.

- Forget the Prozac! Often people who are depressed need to be heard. With depression rampant in our society, you don't have to look far to find someone who needs you to be there for him or her.

4. Comforting the dying.

- Not everyone can be at the bedside of someone who is dying, but if that's your gift, exercising it will be a blessing to many.

5. Forgiving others.

- Talk about a work of mercy that we all can do every day! From family members to co-workers, forgiving those who trespass against us is something we can all do all the time.

As with the financial aspect of almsgiving, the corporal and spiritual works of mercy don't have to be lavish. Inviting a depressed neighbor to dinner can be as important an act as working for Amnesty International. So find something you can do and do it!

SUMMARY   Almsgiving is more than just writing a check for a charity in order to get a tax deduction. True almsgiving is a radical act of faith made concrete, whether it is giving financially or performing one of the corporal or spiritual works of mercy.

Chapter 9

Fasting — Giving Up in Order to Get Closer to God

Fasting

Of all the actions designed to combat our ennui in the spiritual life, fasting is either the easiest or the most difficult because it involves such concrete, measurable activities. Of course, any time we deny ourselves something we want, our human nature objects, but for certain personalities fasting can be easier than for others.

If you are the type of person who likes to know exactly where the lines are drawn and exactly what you have to do right this moment, fasting can be relatively easy. For instance, you decide to fast on Fridays, eating only two simple meals. If it's Friday, you don't eat lunch. Period. What could be simpler?

On the other hand, because it involves very concrete activities, fasting can be extremely difficult for those who prefer to keep their options open at all times. Okay, so it's Friday, but someone offered to take me out to lunch at a restaurant I've been dying to go to. Let's go! I can always fast on Saturday.

No Food, No Drink

Traditionally, fasting refers to giving up food and drink. Catholics of a certain age will remember the proscription against eating meat on Fridays when fasting and abstinence were part of the lexicon of every Catholic family. Today Ash Wednesday and Good Friday are the only official fast days in the Church year (all the Fridays in Lent remain days of abstinence in which meat is not to be consumed).

This does not mean the Church decided fasting on Fridays was a bad idea. No, the Church removed the official law so that the faithful (that's you and me) could have the freedom to choose our own self-discipline. Fasting and abstaining on Fridays is still a good way to begin to wage war against the forces of spiritual boredom.

Expanding the Definition

Fasting usually starts with food and drink, but the concept can and should be expanded to giving up other activities. After all, the whole point of fasting is not just to give up something for the sake of giving it up. The point is to eliminate some things in our life in order to focus more clearly on God and to have more room for God in our lives. With that expanded definition, all of us have a lot of things we can fast from.

For instance, do you and your family watch TV every night? Do you flip it on when you are bored or lonely? Giving up the television (fasting from it) can be a real eye-opener. With the time you save, you might even be able to perform a few more works of mercy!

Here are a few other areas where fasting may be appropriate:

- Not making hobbies a way of life.
- Not making work the goal of life.
- Developing a simple lifestyle.

- Putting away credit cards.
- Buying only what you need, not what you want.
- Giving up little luxuries you now consider necessities.
- Letting someone else have the last word (fasting from always being right).
- Eating lower on the food chain.
- Not buying the latest fashions.
- Not buying CDs, books, or videos.
- Not going to the mall "just to look."

Once you begin to look at your own life, you'll find many other ways to incorporate fasting. After all, it doesn't matter so much *what* you fast from, so long as you introduce the element of fasting into your life.

SUMMARY The third traditional remedy for apathy is fasting — giving up something in order to spend more time with God. Although fasting from food and drink is traditional, one can fast from almost anything.

Chapter 10

Additives for a Modern World

In order for the classical wisdom of prayer, fasting, and almsgiving to give a boost to your spiritual development, we need to add three behavioral elements designed for post-modern times. These elements are necessary because of the pace of our lives and the pressures we so often feel. You might think they are so simple that you don't need to concentrate on them. Please reconsider. Without these additives for a modern world, the time-honored prescriptions will not be as effective nor will your zeal and zest for your faith increase the way you would like it to.

Manage Your Time and Your Life

This is not a time management book. There are a plethora of those lining the shelves of every bookstore. Nor am I going to offer a specific time management technique or tool. Many types of time management tools are available. However, in order to find the time needed for prayer, fasting, and almsgiving, we have to utilize these tools. Without structure to our days, we can end up going to bed having done many urgent things, but few important ones.

There is a classic demonstration in which a person fills a bucket with stones and then asks if the bucket was full. When the audience answers yes, he then pours in several cups full of gravel and again asks if the bucket is full. When his audience again answers yes, he pours in several cups full of sand and again poses this question. This time the audience gets wise and says no as he pours in several ounces of water. The point is well taken. If you don't make time for the big things first, that is, the important things, your life will be filled to the brim with small stuff.

Find a time management tool that suits your lifestyle and begin. Just remember to balance your day between emotional, social, physical, and spiritual activities. And don't forget to keep in mind the reasons you are making these changes in your life.

Reward Yourself

Sometimes Christians get the idea that we should be doing everything out of grim duty. Your responsibility is to suffer now and be rewarded in heaven later. That might work for a few masochistic saints, but for most of us, we need a carrot now and then to keep plugging along. So as you begin to change your behavior, reward yourself by doing something you really like. For example, if you give up your *caffè latte* in order to give money to charity, take a few minutes to appreciate the flock of geese flying overhead or bring in a rose from the garden. If you visit your great-aunt and listen to her stories for three hours, rent a video as a reward. Moreover, don't forget to remind yourself that every time you engage in a new behavior, you increase not only competency and ability, but you are bound to feel good about yourself.

Monitor the Big Picture

This is probably the hardest to do because it requires us to live fully in the present moment and most of us prefer to dwell in the past or the future. But God meets us in the present and that's where we have to live out our lives.

In order to do this, we must do three things.

1. Honor the struggle.

Hey, you're reading this book! You want to make changes in your life. You are doing your best. That's what it means to honor the struggle: you acknowledge that it is difficult to keep your spiritual life filled with fire and zeal, but recognize that you are making overall progress. You give yourself the credit you deserve for trying to improve and not just sitting around lamenting your fate. Remember the old adage: Rome wasn't built in a day and neither can you change long-standing patterns of behavior overnight. Be gentle with yourself and what you are trying to accomplish.

2. Focus on the goal.

You aren't making all these changes just because they seem like a good idea. You are making them so that you will have a deeper, richer, more intimate, and more life-giving relationship with your Creator. As St. Augustine said, "Our hearts are made for Thee, O Lord, and they will not rest until they rest in Thee." Your goal is nothing less than resting in the Lord God Almighty.

3. Count your successes.

Instead of always looking at how far you have to go, remember to take a glance backwards now and then and see how far you have already come. Are you giving more of your time, talents, and material possessions? Wonderful! Are you less angry and more forgiving? Terrific! Remember that God is the author of all of your successes and in acknowledging what you have accomplished, you give him praise and glory.

It sounds easy, but we all know it's not. Let's look at some of the major impediments to rekindling our spiritual zeal and how we can eliminate them.

SUMMARY Modern times need modern methods. Even when dealing with time-honored techniques for recharging your spiritual life, it is important to manage your time, reward your accomplishments, and keep track of the big picture.

Chapter 11

From Apathy to Zest

To change our spiritual lives, we have to have a reason to change. For me, as it is for many who come asking for help, the reason is to rekindle the fires of devotion. Before we can prescribe the cure, however, we must first examine the disease.

Apathy — the lack of zeal or zest — is the core illness in the spiritual lives of many today. Apathy means lack of fire, lack of zeal, and lack of interest. It means settling for what is comfortable. Apathy is simply settling for mediocrity, shying away from the call to greatness. It results from the fast pace of change in everything we do that puts such demands on our lives.

To understand it better, let's turn to a similar period of great change: the Roman world of the fifth century.

The ancient Roman world was crumbling. The barbarians were sweeping across the borders of the Roman Empire, defying imperial authority. The problems in Rome became increasingly complex until administrators were reaching overload. There was too much change coming too fast in every aspect of their life.

It was precisely during this time, with all its turmoil and confusion, that Stoicism became a powerful lifestyle choice. The Stoics basically said that public life was so filled with unpredictable change, so filled with irrational behaviors, and simply so painful, that the best thing to do was to retreat into the "inner sanctuary" of your own villa, your own private life, and bar the doors of your emotions to all others in order to enjoy the last remaining years before the triumph of chaos. The isolation was both personal and social. In order to achieve this, the Stoics said one had to practice what they considered the chief virtue — *apatheia* ("apathy").

The 'Virtue' of Apathy

Today, although we don't claim to elevate apathy to the state of a virtue, we are surrounded by people who act as if it were; sometimes we ourselves act as if it is.

What's going on here? There are three major reasons.

First, in the post-modern world we have been taught to set courage and zeal aside and to compromise.

Zeal and courage are often portrayed as characteristics of religious fanatics and extremists: the religious right, the far left, cults, and radicals. We have been told that there are times when we need to put ourselves first; times when it is necessary to compromise in order to survive in this day and age.

This attitude creates a whole set of attitudes with spiritual effects:

- Why should I bother standing at the cross of the Lord giving the Father control over my life when I am almost powerless as it is?
- Why should I try to help others when nobody else does it?
- Why should I bother doing good when everyone else seems not to care half a whit?

These, in turn, result in our experiencing a downward spiral of unhappiness and frustration. We know we aren't as happy as we should be, but we feel worn down. We know we aren't as full of life for Christ as we could be, but we feel we deserve a break. We know we aren't as zealous as those in Gospel times, but we are too tired to care. As Bishop Fulton Sheen said: "We grow tired of doing good."

In the post-modern age we have not just grown tired. We have been taught to set courage and zeal aside and to compromise. In fact, there is even something called a theology of compromise!

Today we don't have the kind of fire that allowed ordinary men and women to walk as martyrs into the Roman Colosseum. Agnes and Cecilia. Sebastian and Ignatius of Antioch. We don't have the kind of zeal that spread the Gospel from a backwater town in Israel to the ends of the known world.

Instead we have been taught compromise. Zeal for the Lord's house does not consume us. Instead we have been taught toleration and have fallen into indifference.

Nobody wants to suffer from apathy; nobody enjoys being apathetic. Most of us would describe what we are doing as using common sense to survive in a nonsensical world. (Shades of the Stoics!) However, in moments of reflection, we know in our heart of hearts that all too often we compromise in order to live comfortably amid the troubles and trials surrounding the beginning of the third millennium.

We read in the twelfth chapter of Mark's Gospel that we are to love the Lord our God with all our heart, with all our soul, and with all our mind, and all our strength. We are to love our neighbors as ourselves. When we look clearly at our lives we see we have compromised on love. We have become apathetic to the Great Command of Christ.

Sometimes we stand at the foot of the cross of the Lord, but we do not look up in great sadness, touched by his glory. We have become apathetic to the Sacrifice.

We ignore the Resurrection. We feel untouched by its joy. We have become apathetic to the Gift.

In short, we have sold our great heritage for thirty pieces of apathy.

The second reason we have become so apathetic is because we are caught up in our comfort zones.

In an individualistic age, we all have a comfort zone, a matrix or bevy of activities, persons, places, and things we have grown used to and are comfortable with. Outside our comfort zone are all the persons, places, things, and activities we find uncomfortable and that we are not willing to sacrifice for.

Our comfort zones can be understood in terms of thinking, feelings, and behavior.

- I hold certain views about life and religious fervor and I am not inclined to change them. (*Thinking.*)
- There are certain feelings I have grown accustomed to and am not willing to try new ones. (*Feelings.*)
- I am entitled to a comfortable life such as I have and I avoid activities outside my comfort zone of thinking and feeling. (*Behavior.*)

A wonderful example of how comfort zones can get in the way of spiritual development is told in the story of a zealous priest filled with fire for the Lord who volunteered for missionary work in Chile. His bishop said to him: "Your zeal bothers my conscience." But, of course, the zealous priest's zeal didn't bother the bishop's conscience enough for him to break free from his comfort zone.

The third reason for lack of fire and zeal in our spiritual lives is the duping effect of marketing.

Marketing is the art of increasing the number and size of our *wants* and making us believe they are *needs*. If I only had a bigger house, a better car, a bigger salary, a better wardrobe, a better vacation . . . then I would be happy.

The truth is we do not need all these things. We can and should live a simple lifestyle. But the truth has never been popular.

The question "What is truth?" has been answered resoundingly by marketers: "Truth has nothing to do with the buying and selling of happiness in America." Justin the Martyr in the second century wrote about "the scandal of truth." Truth is not popular among marketers today, but it's never been popular among leaders, among rulers, among politicians, among propagandists. Therefore, it is no surprise that it is very unpopular among consumers and those who try to influence them today.

Truth isn't unpopular in just high places. It's not popular among ourselves either.

- We hide the truth about ourselves.
- We rationalize it.
- We deny it.

A brand-new boy came to Girls and Boys Town not too long ago. He was told: "Billy, you have a serious drug problem." He said in response: "I ain't got no problem with drugs. Drugs are not a problem; they are the solution. You're the ones who have got a problem thinking I've got a problem." Billy does not like the truth about himself. Billy is not alone. We don't like the truth about ourselves either. We do not want to know the truth and we surely do not want to practice it because truth might cause us to move beyond our comfort zone.

We believe more in denial than in truth. All we claim we know about denial is (in the words of the famous vaudeville routine): "De Nile is a river in Egypt."

Never Lose Hope

But there is hope.

One of the hopeful characteristics of the post-modern world is that we are increasingly uncomfortable with the compromises that we have made in our lives. We are increasingly uncomfortable with the ways our lives are turning out. We are increasingly uncomfortable with our comfort zones.

A comfort zone is nothing more than "life on my terms." If our comfort zones are working so well, why are so many attracted to New Age spirituality? If our comfort zones are working so well, why are so many dependent on drugs, alcohol, and other addictions? If our comfort zones are working so well, we would only be attracted to Princess Di and not Mother Teresa as well. That feeling of unease with apathy or compromise is very important. More important, it's a feeling you should pay attention to. It's a warning signal that it's not too late to restore your spiritual zest.

So where do we begin?

Step One: Look into your heart to identify the problem.

Start an autobiographical investigation of your feelings of apathy and discomfort with your comfort zone. To begin the process, let the Gospels touch your heart as did the great saints of old: Scholastica, Clare, Catherine of Siena, Francis of Assisi,

Thomas Aquinas, Ignatius of Loyola. Then acknowledge to yourself and to God that there is a problem and ask for help.

Step Two: Change your behavior.

Remember, behavior is easier to control and master than thoughts or feelings.

Starting with behavior takes less of your valuable time. Starting with behavior allows you to more easily develop more strategies and motives.

In our behavioral approach, we enrich the old with the new. We start with the spiritual wisdom of Christianity through twenty long centuries.

SUMMARY Apathy — that is, the lack of zeal or zest — is at the center of spiritual illness plaguing many today. Apathy means lack of fire, lack of zeal, and lack of interest. Apathy means opting for what is comfortable. When we are apathetic, it is impossible to make strides in spiritual development.

Chapter 12

Anxiety — A Major Impediment to Spiritual Advance

One of the major reasons we don't make advances in the spiritual life is because of anxiety. So many of the children at Girls and Boys Town suffer from anxiety disorders that are the result of dysfunctional homes. If a child does not know when she gets up in the morning whether she will get breakfast or a beating, her anxiety is bound to be high. And if it continues month after month, that anxiety is bound to take its toll. Anxiety is a bodily condition like hunger and thirst. It brings wide-sweeping changes in the body as a neurophysiological organic condition.

The Unpredictable and the Uncontrollable

Anxiety is not hard to understand. It is summarized in two basic concepts. The first is "the unpredictable." You don't know what tomorrow will bring. You don't know when you get up in the morning what will happen. Will you be greeted warmly or will someone shout, yell, and scream at you? This is particularly common among victims of abuse, and abuse is growing more common.

What if you are not a victim of abuse? The "unpredictable" still abounds if you live in an unstable environment: freeway traffic, corporate reorganizations, family troubles, stock market gyrations, church in-fighting — to name a few. The more unstable the society is, the more unpredictable it is, and postmodern society is very unpredictable.

This by itself does not create undue anxiety. But anxiety enters when you personally cannot control the unpredictable.

The second idea is "the uncontrollable." Even if I don't know whether I'm going to be greeted by care or violence but do know that I can avoid being the victim of the violence, then I can meet the dawn with a sense of confidence. But if tomorrow is both unpredictable and uncontrollable, then a feeling of helplessness comes over me.

Studies have been done in which people have been subjected to the same amount of pain. Those who felt a sense of helplessness stemming from the combination of the unpredictable and the uncontrollable got more ulcers, were more on edge, and were more likely to find life unpleasant and unrewarding.

Our society is notoriously uncontrollable. Mary Pipher, the author of the best-selling *Reviving Ophelia*, says it well:

> I wouldn't have written this book had it not been for these last few years when my office has been filled with girls — girls with eating disorders, alcohol problems, posttraumatic stress reactions to sexual or physical assaults, sexually transmitted diseases (STDs), self-inflicted injuries and strange phobias, and girls who have tried to kill themselves or run away. A health department survey showed that 40 percent of all girls in my Midwestern city considered suicide last year. The Centers for Disease Control in Atlanta reports that the suicide rate among children age ten to fourteen rose 75 percent between 1979 and 1988. Something

dramatic is happening to adolescent girls in America, something unnoticed by those not on the front lines.

Something similar happens in the lives of boys who increasingly have few if any solid, sound role models of a father or uncle or grandfather who has mastered the art of being a husband and father and to whom a boy can apprentice himself.

Quite apart from dysfunction, even marriage and parenting are much more stressful today because of the shifting social moral norms, as well as social conditions and economic conditions. In the affluent society even poverty is more stressful than in ages past because there is not simply a *desire* for more goods and services, but an *expectation* of them.

Add to that the normal stressful moments: driving to work in rush hour traffic, meeting deadlines, scheduling too many things, and not meeting deadlines.

Even the Church Gets into the Act

Unfortunately, our churches, which should be a bastion of strength against widespread anxiety, often contribute to it. Sunday liturgies have become places where conservative or liberal ideologies are imposed on people at what is meant to be a nourishing spiritual experience of the public prayer of the Church. The ideology of the left or the right is preached much to the detriment of the Gospel. People come to church hungry and leave hungry. It is an anxiety-producing experience in a place where one is promised: "He who eats my flesh and drinks my blood will never hunger or thirst again" (see John 6:54). No wonder people are turning to relaxation methods such as yoga and transcendental meditation as "the way to cope" with an already stressful life.

No wonder many are no longer active in church. Who wants to be disappointed Sunday after Sunday?

The remedy is to trust our heavenly Father, but how do we do that? Trying to trust seems to add, rather than diminish, our anxiety.

Trust in the Lord

Let's look at trusting in the Lord from the triad of thoughts, feelings, and behavior. Spiritual health does not exist in isolation, but is interrelated with four facets of our lives: the physical, the social/emotional, the spiritual, and the mental.

First, we need to reduce the major stressors in our lives. This is a threefold process: identifying what causes the most stress in our lives, developing a behavioral response to each stressor, and, finally, putting the response into action.

For example, a major stressor for Sandra, a married woman with three children, is her mother, who recently entered a nursing home. "I'm the only one who looks after our mother," Sandra explains. "My brother lives in another city and he doesn't have time anyway. My mother calls and regularly puts me down for not being there when she needs me. It makes me so angry and I let her get away with it. Every time I think of her, it ruins my day. Some days I can't get out to see her, and I hate waiting for that call because I know she will be filled with scorn. I'm stuck."

It's not hard to *identify the major stressor* in Sandra's life. Obviously it's her mother, or at least her mother's reaction to being in a nursing home. How can Sandra develop a behavioral response to this common situation? First, she has to say to herself: "This is happening to me because I let it. I am increasingly unhappy because I have been putting up with the situation without trying to change it." It's only after she was ready to make a change that she could begin to create a plan of action.

Sandra *developed a behavioral response* by sitting down and figuring out how many visits a week were realistic and reasonable for her to make with all the other demands on her life. She decided the daily visits were too much. After prayer and thought, she eliminated Tuesdays and Thursdays. Then she decided to eliminate one weekend visit as well, electing to keep Sunday morning so that her mother could have the option of attending Mass with the family. Cutting out Saturdays allowed her to spend more time with her children and her husband.

Sandra then started to *practice the behavior*. She began to feel better that she had a routine that was reasonable and controllable and her family was happy to have her attention. When her mother called and laid a guilt trip on her, Sandra had a friend help her figure out a reasonable response. When she got the dreaded call, Sandra would say, "Mom, I'll be there tomorrow. I love you a whole bunch, but I can't let you put this guilt trip on me. See you tomorrow. Good-bye." She combined this new plan with a little exercise and eating healthy foods (the *physical*), talking more with one of her very best friends (the *social/emotional*), praying with this very specific purpose in mind. The result was that she gained some peace about what she was doing, realizing that it was good, loving, and faithful to God's plan (*spiritual*), and sharing it with others (*mental*) was beneficial.

It's Not the Big Things That'll Kill You

After working on the big stressors of life, it's time to tackle the day-to-day anxieties. These are like aphids, nibbling at the roses of life. If you don't deal with them, sooner or later your prize roses are going to look mighty ragged. Hundreds of books have been written on how to accomplish this, but it's really quite simple.

1. Simplify

A woman I knew not only used to change all the sheets in the house twice a week, she ironed them as well. Clearly this took up a lot of time. Even if her housekeeping standards didn't allow her to cut back on how often she changed the linen, eliminating the step of ironing was a big time-saver. Likewise, you may do things in your life that nibble away at your time, creating stress and anxiety. Take a little time to figure out what they are and then simplify the process.

2. Prioritize

This is the key to every great accomplishment. Do the important things first and let the rest trickle into the available spaces. Make time for God, your family, and your health first. Without these, nothing else matters.

• Do it. In other words, get those priorities done.

• Share your struggle. Nothing helps divide sorrow and share joy more than a good friend.

3. Honor the Struggle

Another important step in reducing or eliminating anxiety – in fact, it is an important step in changing any negative behavior – is to "honor the struggle." In the case of anxiety, this means to set spiritual goals.

Of course our primary goal is heaven, but we can set some intermediate goals along the way. One way to begin is to develop at least one new behavior. These don't have to be profound goals such as starting a soup kitchen or founding a religious order. Rather, they need to be modest, doable goals such as: "I will attend one more Mass a week"; or "I will get to Sunday Church ten minutes ahead of time and really let the Lord touch me"; or "Every day I will compliment my mother on something positive in her life."

Why is honoring the struggle so important? What are we doing when we set spiritual goals?

In a very real sense we are taking back control of our lives. We have stopped acting as if we are powerless before the forces of anxiety and stress in our lives by getting in touch with God our heavenly Father whose love empowers us.

The degree to which we let the love of God empower us is the degree to which we will feel empowered. The way to do this is by sitting (or standing or kneeling or even lying down) in the quiet and opening our hearts to the Lord, letting the Lord love us for at least five minutes every day.

Along with beginning with a new behavior, we also need to complete a weekly examination of conscience. We need to look at whether we are offending the Lord by not taking charge of our own lives, by feeling sorry for ourselves, by being filled with anger and resentment, by accepting our lives as inevitably miserable, by lamenting our fate. The goal of such an examination is, of course, repentance, and repentance means moving beyond today into eternity.

Finally, as we honor the struggle, we need to commit to looking every day for two good things in life and rejoice and enjoy them. Again these don't have to be lottery-winning major events. You might consider telling yourself:

- I will find something good my spouse is doing and praise him or her for it and thank God for it too.

- I will find something happy about the news, or the garden, or my house, or my work, or my family every day.
- I will congratulate myself and do something good for myself for having done so. Maybe I'll treat myself to one hour of reading at nighttime or a nice quiet walk, just something that I really enjoy doing.

It Really Is *What You Do* and Not What You Say

One last word. Some stressors may be so detrimental that the first step in reducing anxiety is to "get out of there." That is the case with so many of our children here at Girls and Boys Town. Even here, children have to learn behavioral responses to remedy the disorder that is destroying their young lives.

By implementing new behaviors in response to the stresses in your life, I believe you will be pleased and surprised at the results. The light of Christ will begin to shine forth more brightly in your life, and your own family and others will notice it and appreciate it and perhaps even imitate you.

A story is told about the late Mother Teresa, who some time ago came to one of her communities in New York. The street in front of the convent where the Sisters of Charity lived was filled with garbage and litter and trash.

Did Mother Teresa blame the people who threw out the garbage for being slobs? Did she call the city and complain? Did she try to overlook the mess? Did she get a migraine fretting over why no one was cleaning? No. She started with behavior — her own. She immediately got a broom and went out in front to clean up the mess and sweep the street.

The people across the street and upstairs in the tenement who had thrown out the garbage in the first place got brooms too. Soon they were out helping her clean it up. The key was to first change the behavior, and then let the thoughts and feelings follow.

The spirit of the Lord shone through Mother Teresa. People saw it and rejoiced in it. Mother Teresa began with behavior. That's a good place for all of us to begin.

SUMMARY One of the major impediments to spiritual growth in our modern age is anxiety. Learning how to reduce anxiety may be the first step in learning how to jump-start our spiritual life.

Chapter 13

Oh, Poor Me —
Envy and Self-Pity

Just as anxiety is a major obstacle to spiritual growth, so is feeling sorry for ourselves. It's unlikely there is a single adult who somehow or other hasn't felt that life dealt him a bad hand. Perhaps he had an alcoholic father or a dysfunctional family. Perhaps it was a missed opportunity for advancement at work. Someone was chosen over him. Someone dumped on him. Life hadn't favored him.

Feeling sorry for ourselves creates a cycle of negativity. Negative thoughts lead to negative feelings that, in turn, lead to negative behavior. The more we think we have been shafted by life (negative thoughts), the more likely we are to have frequent negative feelings about our situation and life itself (blaming others or self). The more we entertain negative thoughts and negative feelings, the more likely we are to do things we are not proud of (negative behaviors).

The Two Sides of Envy

One of the biggest traps of feeling sorry for oneself is that it so often involves envy, one of the seven deadly sins. If we feel sorry for ourselves because we believe life has treated us unfairly, then we can easily become envious of those whom life has favored. We discover a friend has come into an inheritance and we resent our friend's good fortune. We hear about a co-worker's Hawaiian vacation and we begin to dislike that person.

Envy has another side as well. We learn at work that a high-powered co-worker is going away for alcohol rehabilitation. We secretly rejoice. We find out a neighbor who seemed to always have it together is getting a divorce. We gloat. We take secret delight in the misfortunes of those we think life has favored. We rejoice in evil.

That's what envy is — rejoicing in evil. It is sneering. It is sly. It is vicious. It always looks for the worst. In Dante's *Divine Comedy*, the envious in purgatory suffer terribly. Their eyelids are permanently shut until entry into heaven. As the poet tells us: "The envious could not bear to look upon joy and rejoice in happiness in this life. So in purgatory for a while, their eyes are closed so that they cannot see the joy of the resurrection."

The ways feeling sorry for ourselves and becoming envious affect our lives are clear. We feel restless, slowed down, fatigued. Nothing much matters and nothing much counts. Once that happens, our prayer life becomes dry. We simply go through the motions. Then, as we grow into old age, where one's options are only dignity or despair, we choose despair. We become despondent. We begin to say to ourselves, "I spent all my life working. And now that I am old, what is my lot? They put me out to pasture. It's too hot in the summer with too little food and it's too cold in the winter with too little warmth. Nobody loves me. Everybody hates me. I'm going out and eat worms."

Behavioral spirituality says simply that the best place to start remedying the situation is with positive behavior. Positive behavior, if persisted in long enough, will generally result in positive feelings and positive thoughts.

What's the Remedy?

What is the cure to the collection of illnesses created by the "poor me" syndrome? Rather than a remedy, behavioral spirituality suggests two questions: Do you want to be healed by the Lord? Are you willing to *do* what is necessary?

You must honestly answer these questions. Naaman the Syrian wanted to be healed of his leprosy (see 2 Kings 5). But the prophet Elisha told him to engage in behavior he thought was useless — washing seven times in the Jordan River. Then the question was asked again, "Naaman, do you want to be healed by the Lord or not?" The same question is asked of each of us.

If the answer is yes, then behavioral spirituality suggests a set of actions that will allow the Lord's healing to come into your life.

The triad of thinking, feeling, and behavior comes into play again:

1. Getting to work helping others.
2. Coping with sad feelings through daily prayer.
3. Thinking new thoughts.

Let's look at each of them individually.

1. Getting To Work Helping Others

This involves moving from inactivity to activity in the presence of the Lord. It involves three steps.

The first is to create a working plan.

Figure out what you would like to do:

- Visit the sick.
- Call a shut-in.
- Volunteer at your church or civic organization, etc.

If you think you can't do anything, think again. There always is a way to help others, no matter what our condition if we have the determination to find it.

A good example is a retired priest, seventy-five years old, who had serious surgery and was feeling pretty sorry for himself. When I suggested that he develop a work plan, he said, "I can't do anything." It is true that he can't do much physically. He has a hard time walking and can't drive. He can't actually go out and work with others.

But his phone is right in his living room. I suggested that he call one shut-in every day to chat with and cheer up. He started doing this and was amazed that even he could have a ministry. He now says: "I *can* do something." Notice that his thinking changed because his behavior changed!

Second, carry out your plan one day at a time.

This simply means concentrating on today, not on the past or the distant future. If you can help someone today, that's enough. After all, today is all we really have. Yesterday is past and tomorrow is in God's hands.

Finally, share the success of your plan with another caring adult.

Why do you want to do this? In order to be able to see what's going on in your life. That way, when someone asks how you are and what you did today, your response can be: "I visited Mrs. Smith and she seemed so happy." You will begin to recognize the changes in your feelings when you see them reflected back by someone else.

2. Coping Through Daily Prayer

Almost nothing banishes negative feelings better than daily prayer. This isn't just a quick "Our Father" or a pious thought. This is hard-core praying! For this kind of daily prayer, use a

Bible, a prayer book, or the Divine Office, something tangible and concrete, as an aid.

As you begin your prayer, identify the situations that are contributing to your negative feelings. For instance, allow yourself to acknowledge that you still haven't gotten over your grief over your mother's death.

Accept the feelings as they arise. Sometimes you may have to think a bit to figure out exactly what you are feeling. Are you angry? Disappointed? Frustrated? Sad? You can't accept the feelings until you identify them.

Next, use your prayer aid. Choose a passage of Scripture, a favorite prayer — maybe one from the saints — or the daily readings of the Office. Read slowly and attentively, making the reading into a heartfelt prayer.

Now focus on the feelings of closeness and peace that come from the readings. Remember the words of Scripture: The Lord is close to the brokenhearted. He binds up all their wounds (see Psalm 147:3).

Finally, concretize your experience. You could talk about it with a caring peer, but journaling can be even more effective. Why is writing about your feelings helpful? Because the very act of putting your thoughts on paper can help rid yourself of the negative thoughts that enhance negative feelings. It's one way to "flush" negativity and allow the love of the Lord to fill your heart.

3. Thinking New Thoughts

The final step in curing the "poor me" syndrome is to think new thoughts. This involves three steps.

First, be aware of negative thinking.

Get in touch with your pattern of negative thinking. Realize that you are allowing negativity to dominate your thoughts.

The first step to conquering the enemy is to figure out where the enemy is!

Second, think new thoughts.

Find a way to create new thoughts. Guess what? The best way is through changing behavior, not trying to change your thoughts per se. How about using this triad?

- I will get to work helping others.
- I will deal with my sad feelings through prayer.
- I will avoid focusing on negative thoughts.

In other words, you will emulate the Lord by doing his deeds, and praying his prayers. As a result, you will begin to think his thoughts.

Third, honor your struggle.

Honoring your struggle with regards to feeling sorry for yourself means that you allow yourself to be pleased with the efforts that you are making to overcome evil by doing good. It's not an easy struggle. But it is an important one, and you are on the offensive. Give yourself some credit!

Just Do It!

I tell the following story every August at Girls and Boys Town when we begin a new school year.

Mrs. Murphy was a schoolteacher, a very good one, indeed. She loved her preschool children, each and every scruffy one of them.

One summer her mother died, and although she didn't know it at the time, it took an enormous emotional toll on her. All she knew was that she felt tired all the time. She felt very tired. She felt as if the meaning had gone out of her life. She did not look forward to the start of school in late August. In fact, she almost dreaded it.

The first week back in school was an unhappy one. Mrs. Murphy was impatient and cross with the children. She felt resentful at the happy faces of her children. And, of course, the children seemed so unresponsive and so unconcerned about her needs.

On Monday of the second week of school, five-year-old Maria brought a little bouquet of garden flowers to her. She presented them with these words: "Mrs. Murphy, you used to be like a mother. I hope these flowers will help you be like a mother again."

Mrs. Murphy was surprised, "Maria, what is a mother like?"

Maria said: "A mother is what you used to be like. A mother likes being with children."

Mrs. Murphy tried to explain that she was out of sorts because her mother died, and she was shocked when little Maria said in reply: "Did she live until she died?"

Mrs. Murphy answered "Everybody lives until they die, Maria."

Maria said, "Oh, no, they don't. Some people die while they're still alive. Please, Mrs. Murphy, don't die just because your mother did. Stay alive."

That night, Mrs. Murphy stopped feeling so very sorry for herself. She still felt the loss of her mother, but she decided to live until she died.

We all must do the same.

SUMMARY Feeling sorry for ourselves creates a cycle of negativity that leads to negative thoughts. These lead to negative feelings that, in turn, lead to negative behavior. The more we think life has been unfair to us (negative thoughts), the more likely we are to harbor negative feelings about our situation and life itself (blaming ourselves or others). The more we entertain negative thoughts and negative feelings, the more likely we are to indulge in negative behaviors.

Chapter 14

You Make Me So Mad!
Anger As an Obstacle to Growth

Just as feeling sorry for ourselves is a major obstacle to spiritual growth, so too is anger. As we enter the twenty-first century, anger has become a lifestyle for many. Children are angry at their parents, whether they are dead or alive. Parents are angry at their children and their spouses. Spouses are angry at each other. Workers are angry at their employers. Employers are angry at the government. Environmentalists are angry at the polluters. Feminists are angry at a male-dominated society. Victims are angry at their victimizers. This list goes on and on.

The anger many feel borders on rage. A sixteen-year-old boy, Geraldo, walked into the sacristy as I was getting ready for Mass and said, "Father, is it okay to hate your mother?" He had some industrial-strength reasons for doing so. His alcoholic prostitute mother abandoned him and his six brothers and sisters. They were found eating garbage in the streets of El Paso. Geraldo had a frequent dream in which his mom put all the kids in a station wagon, parked on a railroad track, locked them in, and abandoned them as a fast freight train was approaching. I said to Geraldo, "Yes, it is okay to hate your mother. But I wouldn't do it long because it will destroy you." That's the kind of anger that is so prevalent today.

When we were young, we used to say, "Sticks and stones can break my bones, but words can never hurt me." We all know how untrue that is. Cruel words spoken in anger can destroy a relationship more quickly than anything else. A mom can tell her children ninety-nine times that she loves them. All she has to say once is: "I hate you." That's what her kids will remember. It doesn't matter that alcohol, sickness, bitterness, or cynicism was behind the words. All that matters are the hateful words.

A Way to Be in Control

Anger is directly related to power and its use or misuse. The issue of power and anger is the issue of being in control. Pilate needed to be in control. To accomplish this, he ordered the crucifixion of our Savior and Lord. Judas needed to be in control. In order to accomplish this, he betrayed our Lord and Savior and hanged himself. To embrace the cross, Jesus had to cease being in control. He had to let go and do the will of his heavenly Father: "Father, . . . if you are willing, take this cup away from me. Nevertheless, let your will be done, not mine" (Luke 22:42, *Jerusalem Bible*; see also Matthew 26:39 and Mark 14:36).

Being angry with others keeps us from following the Lord. Being angry about past hurtful events keeps us from doing God's will. Anger keeps us from embracing the cross. Just as without surrendering control, Jesus could not have been the firstborn from the dead, so too without our surrendering control, we cannot be reborn into eternal life.

Anger's First Cousin

Cynicism is anger's first cousin. Nothing is more corrosive to human flourishing than constant biting cynicism, no matter whether in a family, office or school, convent or rectory. Cynicism is at the heart of the demonic in modern society.

Take, for example, what happens when a teenager indulges in cynical behavior. She finds nothing good in what her parents do (negative thoughts). She is reinforced by peers who are equally cynical (more negative thoughts). She listens to music that reinforces the cynicism (negative feelings). She laughs at dark humor (more negative feelings). She engages in cynical behavior (negative behavior).

When a teenager opens his or her heart more than an inch to anger and cynicism, there is room for nothing else. For a cynical teenager to change, there first has to be a change in — guess what? — behavior. Once the teenager begins to behave in a more positive, more loving, more optimistic manner, the cynicism will begin to fade away.

Anger, Cynicism, and Victim Mentality

In recent years, anger and cynicism have taken a new form, one that revolves around "victim status." The sophistry of this new approach is enormously seductive. Let's look at three examples.

A twice-divorced and remarried woman in her sixties is extremely angry at the Church she grew up in. Through "the repressive deceit of puritanical nuns and celibate clergy," she feels cheated out of the opportunity for normal sexual growth and development.

A very conservative young man in his thirties is angry at the Church he grew up in. Through the wicked designs of liberal theologians, certain facts were hidden from his view, namely, the intentional "misdesign" of liturgical reformers to destroy belief in the Real Presence of the Lord in the Eucharist and the attempt to force women priests on the Church by deliberately fostering a vocation crisis.

A woman in her forties is angry to the core. "Through twenty centuries of deceit and hypocrisy by every Christian denomination," she and all others have been cheated out of knowing that all the Christian churches are way off base. A higher form of consciousness is breaking upon the world in this "New Age."

The common message in all three of these is the same:

- You have been cheated out of a big chunk of life.
- You have missed truly formative experiences.
- You were denied what you had a right to.
- You were lied to.
- Your bitterness is a just response to these outrages.

Cynicism lies at the base of all these messages.

Cynicism Within the Faith

Many Catholics on the far left feel they have been completely cheated by the oppression, domination, subjugation, and subordination of a male, celibate, homophobic, hierarchical elite. They believe this sophistry. Their cynicism is despair on parade.

Similarly, so many right-wing Catholics feel they have been cheated out of their God-given ecclesiastical heritage by cunning liberal bishops who have an agenda bent on destroying Holy Mother Church through lies and duplicities.

Many Christians of various denominations feel cheated by their past that was — by their own reckoning — either too conservative or too liberal. It makes them angry. It makes them feel like victims and that, in turn, makes them cynical. They feel that cynicism gives them a sense of independence, of control, of power in the midst of their feelings of powerlessness.

But the fact is that to redeem us, Jesus had to let go of control. He had to do the will of his heavenly Father. To embrace the cross, Jesus had to cease being in control.

'Your Will, Not Mine'

As we enter the third millennium of Christianity, we have to give up our anger and our cynicism. We need to move beyond our childhood dependence and our adolescent independence and righteous indignation. We have to move into the interdependence of adulthood in a culture that values only independence.

The Gospels tell us that our Savior and Lord put his life, his independence, in the hands of his Father in the midst of some exceedingly cynical, hateful, and spiteful people who interpreted his behavior, thoughts, and feelings in the most negative light. They asked, "Can any good come out of Nazareth?" (See John 1:46.) They claimed, "It is by the Prince of Devils that he casts out devils" (see Luke 11:18). They demanded, "By whose power and authority do you do this?" (See Luke 9:1.)

What was Christ's response? "If it be possible, let this chalice pass from me, not my will but thine be done" (see Matthew 26:39, Mark 14:36, and Luke 22:42).

Jesus wants us to surrender power to our heavenly Father. That surrender is not based on feelings, but on faith and reason. To satisfy our spiritual hunger, we have to do the will of our heavenly Father in the midst of churches that are divided by liberal and conservative ideologies. Extremists in both groups are fighting for control, and not surprisingly, many of them are filled with a terrible anger.

The Nitty Gritty

Let us look at how we can put aside the anger and cynicism that prevent us from having the richly rewarding spiritual life God wants to give each of us.

First, learn how to control angry behavior.

Each person who struggles with anger needs to pick and choose, among the various anger-control strategies, one or two that is found helpful. Some possibilities include taking a five-minute time-out, counting to ten, writing a letter (but not mailing it), and deep breathing.

Second, get in touch with hot buttons, events that trigger angry feelings.

Here are just a few things that set people off:

- Church people preaching an ideology not your own.
- Media interviews with self-styled authorities belittling your views.
- Solicitors calling your home.
- Politicians embracing religious and moral views opposite to yours.
- Relatives putting down things you hold sacred.
- Inattention to details by peers or subordinates.
- People talking behind your back.
- Unsolicited advice.
- People who talk too much.
- People who mouth off to you.
- Comments about your physical appearance.
- Parental complaints that haven't changed in twenty years.
- Spousal complaints that haven't changed in twenty years.
- Not being listened to.
- Someone embarrassing you.
- Doing something stupid.

Third, recognize what feelings precede the feeling of anger.

For example, if someone makes a comment about your appearance, do you feel hurt? Belittled? Ashamed? If others try to force their viewpoint on you, do you feel frustrated? Denigrated?

As you look more deeply at the feelings that precede anger, you also need to ask if you are reacting appropriately to the situation. For example, if the person telling you that you are stupid is drunk, then becoming outraged may be overkill. Just shrugging off the comment may be the better reaction.

A New Thinking Pattern

Often you can help negative feelings pass by recognizing them and not letting them take control. You might use some practical self-talk to dissipate the feelings before they burst into anger. If you are unfamiliar with the way to create a new thinking pattern, it's not as difficult as it might seem.

Step 1: Try some new behaviors.

(Where have we heard that before!) Positive behaviors, if engaged in long enough, tend to develop positive feelings and positive thoughts. It takes a while for these positive feelings and positive thoughts to come forward and gain the day, but of course, it took a while for anger to dominate our thoughts and behaviors as well.

A few behaviors that can help might include giving compliments, accepting compliments without cynicism, laughing at oneself, and being willing to compromise.

Step 2: Become aware of your negative thought patterns.

This is nothing more than becoming aware of how you distort reality. There are many distortions, but three are the most common.

Filtering. This means focusing on thoughts that correspond to our feelings. In other words, a person who is feeling quite sorry for himself views the world through hopeless- and powerless-colored glasses. He carefully chooses to pay attention to those things that reinforce his notion that the world is a very bad place, indeed. Another example is a person who brings up all the sad memories of childhood, to the exclusion and sometimes even denial of any happy ones, so that she can justify her feelings of worthlessness.

Catastrophising. This might be called the "Chicken Little" syndrome. Every little fear or disappointment is a disaster. For instance, a newlywed couple has a fight and they conclude divorce is looming on the horizon. A student gets a C on the first test of a course, and concludes he is flunking. It rains on the first day of a family vacation, so the entire week is considered ruined.

Overgeneralization. This is the thought process that projects the future based on one or two past events. For example, a woman whose fiancé breaks their engagement may conclude she will never love or be loved again. A student who does poorly his first semester at college may conclude he wasn't cut out for higher education.

This distortion is very seductive and can be very difficult to detect because it is inbred by our culture: It's a dog-eat-dog world. The golden rule is "them that has the gold makes the rules." Life is unfair, so deal with it. It requires concentrated prayer and sometimes the help of a professional counselor to help spot this particular negative thought pattern.

Step 3: Replace negative thought patterns with positive ones.
This is where those of us with faith in the Lord have a great advantage. We have the promise of Jesus that those who leave everything behind and follow him will receive a hundredfold in

this life and eternal life in the next. We know this isn't the end of the line. There is a final chapter, and the good guys win . . . by trusting in the Lord.

To help combat negative thinking, you might want to write one or more of the following thoughts on an index card and post them where you can see them regularly. The more often you see and read these truths, the deeper they will sink into your inner being where they can change your life.

- The Lord gave control over his life to his heavenly Father and wants me to do the same.
- Giving control to God is not the dependence of childhood.
- God wants me to open myself to his spirit and life and become dependent on his guidance.
- Only by giving up my power, all of my power, can the power of God take over my life.
- "Be a good soldier of Jesus Christ" (see 2 Timothy 2:3).

Don't Let Anger Win

A dear friend of mine named Ruthie was born and raised in Cologne, Germany, in the 1930s. Her father was a dentist. They were Jewish, and everyone in the family perished in the Holocaust except Ruthie. Today she is one of the happiest people I have ever met; she is good-natured, outgoing, and caring of others.

I asked her one day, "Ruthie, why aren't you angry? Why doesn't hate consume your life?"

Her response is a lesson. She said, "If I opened the door of my heart this far [she indicated an inch with her fingers] to anger, I wouldn't have room for anything else."

She is right. Don't let anger win. Shut the door on it today.

SUMMARY Just as feeling sorry for ourselves is a major obstacle to spiritual growth, so too is anger. As we enter the twenty-first century, anger has become a lifestyle for many, a lifestyle that does not permit true spiritual maturity.

Chapter 15

Who Me? Lie?

One of the most insidious ways we stymie our relationship with God is by telling ourselves "little lies." These are an outgrowth of negative feelings that allow us to continue with our negative behaviors. These little lies keep us in mediocrity, surrounded by fear and anxiety, and locked in depression.

Here are just a few examples of the kinds of "little lies" I hear from the children and families we try to help at Girls and Boys Town:

- My family is a bunch of dysfunctional alcoholics, and there is no sense fighting addiction in my own life.
- Everybody does drugs, sex, and alcohol, so why sweat it?
- No one in my family graduated from college, so who do I think I am?
- People who strive for holiness are nuts and flakes. Take Jimmy Swaggart, for example.
- My dad says: "A little infidelity never hurt anybody."
- "A little shoplifting never hurt anybody."
- "A little sexual harassment of classmates never hurt anybody."

If you tell yourself little lies often enough, you soon lose touch with truth itself. Likewise, if you engage in negative behaviors long enough, you soon lose touch with the desirability of good behavior. If you wallow in negative feelings long enough, positive feelings will eventually seem foreign and strange.

Telling ourselves little lies not only prevents us from seeing the truth, it also keeps us from being free. There is an intimate relationship between truth and freedom that can be seen in the story of the alcoholic who kept telling himself: "There is nothing wrong with my drinking." If he does not know that he is powerless before alcohol, he cannot possibly attain freedom. If he does not know that the only road away from addiction is to get in touch with a Higher Power, he will never be free from the chemicals that control his body.

Telling ourselves little lies is a terrible obstacle to becoming really free.

Lying Does Make a Difference

A prime example of what happens when we allow little lies to infiltrate our lives is shown in the story of Pam, twelve, who arrived at Girls and Boys Town having been shot by her father. He was a common drunk with a terrible temper. The little lies he told himself were: "A little alcohol won't hurt anybody." "I can always stop if I want to." "I have a tough job and need to relieve the tension." He told himself those little lies so often that he gradually lost touch with all truth itself.

He came home drunk one night, got in a fight with his wife, dragged her outside and beat her against the pickup truck so badly that she is paralyzed from the waist down. Then he shot his daughter, not once but five times. She was lucky she survived.

Little Lies?

Little lies. Pontius Pilate was a master at telling himself little lies. As the emperor's representative in a backwater province called

Palestine, he had to keep the peace in an explosive political situation, never quite understanding what these Jews were up to. And if he was successful in this dismal place, he might be promoted. It wasn't much of a command, but at least it was a command.

When Jesus was brought before him, Pilate asked: "Are you the King of the Jews?" (Matthew 27:11; see also Mark 15:2, Luke 23:3, and John 18:33).

To paraphrase the Gospel of John, Jesus answered: "Does this question come from you or have others told you about me?"

Pilate said: "What's the matter? Do you think I am a Jew? It was your own people, led by the chief priest, who handed you over to me. What have you done?"

And Jesus replied: "My kingdom does not belong to this world. If my kingdom belonged to this world, my followers would fight to keep me from being handed over to the Jews. My kingdom does not belong here."

And Pilate said: "Then you are a king?"

And Jesus answered: "You have said it. I am a king. I was born into this world for this one purpose, to speak about the truth. Whoever belongs to the truth listens to me."

Pilate's telling response is: "What is truth?" Pilate had told himself so many little lies that he had gradually lost touch with truth altogether. Thus he could say in contempt: "What is truth?" Who cares? It doesn't matter. Only power and advancement matter.

When the people intimidated Pilate by crying: "If you do not crucify him you are no friend of Caesar," he fell back on the little lies he had told himself over and over:

- You can't buck the system.
- You have to look out for yourself.
- You can't risk your career on one case.

- You have to worry about what Rome will say.
- Put yourself first.

So he could, with typical Roman arrogance, assure this upstart Jesus that talking about truth was for the naïve, for the simple-minded, for the unsophisticated, and that he had no interest in the question. If a person can do that, then he or she honestly does not have any hold on truth at all. There is just none left.

And then with impunity, you can get rid of Jesus by washing your hands and ordering him to Golgotha, then getting on with more important matters.

The little lies we tell ourselves are walls that surround our comfort zone. They help to keep our consciences from being troubled. We don't like others to lie to us. But we lie to ourselves all the time . . . so our consciences won't be troubled.

Yet trouble us they do. We hunger for something more than another beer or another day at the beach. We avoid a little pain. We neglect a little goodness.

What can we do to change?

Unlearning the Lies of Life

First and foremost we must start telling ourselves the truth as seen through the eyes of faith. Like the blind man in the Gospel, we can see only a little at first. But the more Jesus touches us, the clearer our sight becomes. To start telling the truth requires learning three new skills . . . in addition to our life of prayers.

1. Sorting Out Feelings

Distorted thinking says that what we feel must always be true. How can you tell whether your feelings are true or not?

By examining them to see if they are appropriate or inappropriate. By seeing if they are in accord with what is really so or not. By seeing if they are based on exaggerated fears or falsehood. In other words, by seeing whether they are responsive to ontic values or not. Ontic values are the values of being in a right relationship with God and our neighbor in the areas of truth, goodness, beauty, and being itself. A good friend can help us in this task.

2. Distinguishing Clear Thinking from Emotional Reasoning

So many of our emotions are the product of emotional reasoning that says if you feel something, it must be true. For instance, if you feel guilty, you must be guilty. If you don't feel guilty, you must not be guilty. The trial of O. J. Simpson illustrates this point. Despite what the civil court found, he doesn't feel guilty; therefore, he can't be guilty. A friend can help here too.

3. Analyzing Your Personal Truths

This cannot be accomplished without prayer and hard work. Scrutinize the personal truths or the things you believe to be true in your life by putting them to the test of God's Word. Study it, understand it, and apply it under the direction of the Holy Spirit. Begin to look at your own truths by praying, "Teach me your truths, O Lord, that I may gain wisdom of heart." I know many bright students whose "personal truth" is this: "I'm so smart I don't have to work too hard." They are just plain lazy.

Learn the Words to Your Song

The second aspect of change is to discover and accept the unique mission and purpose God has for your life. Most of us just sort of live life as it happens, not realizing that we are here, sent by God on a special mission. The Son of God was sent by the Father on a mission to earth. Each of us is "missioned" by God.

- Each of us has a message to deliver that we alone can deliver.
- Each of us has a song to sing that we alone can sing.
- Each of us has a love to bring that we alone can bring. In the end it is good to remember that while all human beings are called by God to know him, love him, and to serve him in our brothers and sisters, each one of us has a very specific and very individual mission. If we do not achieve the purpose for which God put us on this earth, there will be something very much lacking in God's plan of creation and redemption.
- Each of us has a love to give to particular people. If we do not love them or serve them, harm will come into their lives.
- Each one of us is called to deliver a specific message to specific people at a specific time and in a specific place. If we do not deliver it, it will simply not be seen or heard.
- Each one of us is called to sing a song particular to our time and to our place and to our audience. If we do not sing it, there will be less beauty in the world.

If we do not do what we are called to do, it will never be done.

In the past, if you gave up trying to figure out what specific mission the good Lord has put you on this earth for, it is time to redouble your efforts to do so.

Here are some ways to begin.

First, start an autobiographical investigation beginning with when you were a child in your own family in order to search out what the good Lord has called you specifically to do. God has destined you for union with him and others in him. But how?

Second, repent of the lies you have told yourself regarding your abilities, your faults, your failures, your life.

Third, begin today by behaving in a manner appropriate to the mission the Lord has you on. You can tell whether your behaviors are appropriate if they are in accord with the Ten Commandments, if they are in accord with the Profession of Faith and the Creed, and if they are in accord with the duties of your state of life. For instance, long hours spent in contemplation before the Blessed Sacrament is appropriate to a cloistered nun. It is not appropriate for a wife and mother. St. Francis de Sales taught us that long years ago.

In other words, start carrying out the mission God has sent you on.

The Truth of Fiction

As a young student in Europe, I was very much taken with the novels of Morris West. One of his early novels was called *The Devil's Advocate*. Set in Rome, it focuses on the life of Monsignor Blase Meredith who has been a priest for twenty years. He has just been told he has cancer and doesn't have long to live. Yet, he doesn't find great consolation in his faith, now that the date of his departure is set.

In fact, he is shocked at how unnerved he has become and how unready he is. Why? After all, he has spent his whole life working comfortably and successfully in the Roman Curia. He has been an Auditor in the Sacred Congregation of Rites. He has been the personal assistant to the Prefect of the Congregation, Eugenio Cardinal Miratta. Still he was unhappy. Still he was unprepared to go because he has told himself little lies. And oh, how he has cherished them. What lies has he cherished? "I know what life is," he tells himself. "Life is a good job in Rome. Life means never wanting to have more than is available to me. I sit in the councils of the Pope. I have a nice apartment. I have good meals. I am comfortable and content. It is enough."

The author says it this way: "Monsignor Meredith never planted a tree. He never set a stone on another for a house or a monument. He spent no anger, dispensed no charity. No poor would ever bless him for their bread. No sick would bless him for their courage. No sinners would bless him for their salvation. He had done everything that was demanded of him, yet he would die empty. And within a month, his name would be a blown dust on the desert of the centuries."

No wonder he was terrified of death. His lies had left him empty of life.

What happened to him? Morris West says he was "deficient in sympathy." I like that. He was deficient behaviorally . . . in the corporal and spiritual works of mercy.

In the final days of his life, he went to southern Italy. There he helped a troubled priest return to the faith. He took a child out of harm's way. He brought light to a lost and unhappy woman. When he died he asked to be buried with the people of the obscure town where he moved, saying: "I have found myself as a human being and as a priest."

What did he do? He quit telling himself little lies. He started with new behavior and ultimately he found himself and God.

SUMMARY One of the most insidious ways we stymie our relationship with God is by telling ourselves "little lies." These are an outgrowth of negative feelings that allow us to continue with our negative behaviors. These little lies keep us in mediocrity, surrounded by fear and anxiety, and locked in depression.

Chapter 16

Bitterness and Its Natural Cure

As we look at those things that prevent us from having the kind of zest-filled, joyous spiritual life we want, we cannot overlook the pervasive bitterness that is a part of so many lives and its natural cure — forgiveness.

What is forgiveness and how can it positively affect our spiritual development? Let's start with a little introduction of what forgiveness is and what it isn't.

Forgiveness

Forgiveness is a very ancient way of making amends. All the great literature of the past — Hindu, Greek, Jewish, Roman, you name it — stresses the importance of forgiveness. The fact is human beings cannot flourish without it because forgiveness and repentance are the only ways to resolve the guilt we have within us. They are the only way to resolve the resentments people and nations have and the terrible self-torture we suffer.

Forgiveness has nothing to do with the popular fundamentalist idea that we often see paraded on television. Take, for example, a family whose daughter has been raped. The camera crew sticks a microphone in front of her parents and asks them how they feel. Dad says, "Oh, I forgive him in the name of Jesus."

These are empty words, folks! This is not the reality of for-giveness! I am sure the person who says these words is a won-derful person, but forgiveness is not encapsulated in these words. Forgiveness has to do with a complex interchange be-tween thinking, feeling, and behaviors.

A more honest response for the dad at that moment would probably be: "I would like to kill that person if I catch him." Forgiveness is a process, not an event. And this is a more hon-est beginning on the long, long road to forgiveness.

Forgiveness also isn't something that can be summarized in a sound bite. When President Clinton went to Africa, he said that he was truly sorry that the American citizens played a terrible part in African slavery. However nice that sounded, there wasn't a bit of change in his thinking, his feelings, or behavior; nor was there a bit of change in the thinking, feeling, and behaviors of the American people. This is not repentance or forgiveness. It is political marketing.

What Forgiveness Requires

As children we don't know how to repent or how to for-give, and unfortunately many adults don't know how either. The first step in understanding what forgiveness requires is understanding who needs to repent.

1. It's simple: the guilty repent.

There is a difference between a sin and an error. Lying is a sin. Believing two plus two equals five is an error. The remedy for an error or mistake is education . . . learning that two plus two equals four. The remedy for sin is repen-tance. Pope John Paul II apologized for the Roman Catho-lics of Europe who willingly took part in the Holocaust in

World War II. He wisely said that simply stating an apology is not repentance or forgiveness. Rather, repentance is a long and involved process that evidences visible change in the feelings, actions, and behavior of an individual over a long period of time.

Where does behavioral spirituality say the process of forgiveness begins? We begin with our behavior. We kneel before the Lord, acknowledge our sin (not just errors or mistakes), and ask his forgiveness. Then we start to build positive relationships day by day, doing positive things for others, asking forgiveness, saying we're sorry, and really caring for one another.

Teshuvah is the Hebrew word for repentance. It literally means a "response." As a response, it involves a change of character. By the process of *teshuvah* you are changed; you become another person. The change involves a change of heart and mind. We Christians call this change, or transformation, *metanoia*.

2. Make restitution.
Another element marks true forgiveness – restitution.

If you steal fifty dollars from me and come and say, "I'm really sorry and I'm confessing to you that I stole it and I'm asking you to forgive me," I am going to naturally ask, "Where is my money?" If you just ask for forgiveness and make no effort to restore what you have taken, your words are a sham. Restitution is an integral part of forgiveness.

I see so many victims of physical, emotional, and sexual abuse among our children. And often an abusive parent will go through therapy, show up at my doorstep, and ask his child to forgive him . . . without making any effort at restitution.

For example, a father sexually abused his daughter since the third grade. She ended up being involved in drugs, alcohol, sex, truancy, and stealing by age thirteen when she came to us. She is fragile and on the road to recovery . . . afraid of the man who took away her childhood, her happiness, her innocence. She shoulders the burden of pain and recovery. He shows up and puts another burden on her: forgiveness. I always tell such a fellow: "Before you ask forgiveness, make restitution. Give your daughter back what you stole from her. How? By helping her understand it was you who groomed her, you who made her feel guilty, you who helped her want more, you who ruined her life." This is the beginning of restitution. Without it, he should stay away. And he has to continue making restitution all his life.

Purification of the Heart

Without forgiveness, given to those who have hurt us and asked of those whom we have hurt, we can never have the kind of spiritual life we long for because the pain we harbor will hamper our relationship with everyone we contact.

Ultimately, purification of the heart is central to real forgiveness and true Christian zeal. We must come to our God and say, "Father, I have sinned against heaven and against you. It is my fault. I open my heart to you." Purification of the heart means that you go through a period of mourning. You can share it with others, but you have to go through it yourself. It takes a long time until one day you wake up and say: "I've mourned enough." In our Christian tradition, the mourning always comes before rejoicing, just as the darkness of night always comes before the light of morning!

SUMMARY Without forgiveness — that gift we offer to those who have hurt us and asked of those whom we have hurt — we can never expect to have the kind of spiritual life we long for because the pain we harbor, the resentment we allow to eat at us, will prevent us from building up a good relationship with those we need to make amends.

Chapter 17

A Closing Thought — What's in It for Me?

The goal of life is union with God and others in God. This is what God asks of you, "to act justly, to love tenderly and to walk humbly with your God" (Micah 6:8, *Jerusalem Bible*).

The purpose of existence couldn't be put more simply. We are on the journey to see our Father face to face, and we must love and help one another on this journey, ensuring that we bring each other home.

We are here so that we can form an intimate personal relationship with God and others in God, a relationship that will last through all eternity. Most of us, however, never quite achieve that degree of spirituality or closeness to God that we would like.

Behavioral spirituality is one way that we can begin to make more progress in that direction. It is a way to have a more powerful, more personal, more vibrant relationship with God. I've seen the enormous changes behavioral spirituality can make in the lives of both adults and children, and I know it will make a difference in your life. As I've stressed through this little book, behavioral spirituality starts with behavior – what you actually do! It doesn't matter where you are in your spiritual journey, you can always do something – even if it's just making a phone call or some other small beginning.

Beginning with behavior means you can see results right away. If you begin fasting or giving to charity, you see and feel an immediate change. You don't have to wait a lifetime to see the effects.

As I've said over and over, changing our behavior changes our thoughts and feelings. You can't think the same thoughts when you don't act the same way. It's just not possible, except through denial. Once you alter your behavior, you will sooner or later alter the way you look at life. And when you alter the way you look at life, you alter the way you will feel about life.

A Reasonable Question

What happens if you change your behavior and you don't begin to feel differently? What's going on if you continue to have the same old thoughts and feelings although you've made a concerted effort to alter your behaviors? It's a reasonable question and one best answered by an example.

Let's say you begin to work out. You can't expect to have a rock-hard body after only one session. It takes time; time to get your muscles accustomed to exercise, time to lose the flab, time to reshape your body. In fact, in the beginning you'll probably feel more tired and less energetic than you did when you were a couch potato. Muscles you never even knew you had will ache and you may be sorely tempted to give up.

That's when the adage "Practice makes perfect" comes into play. You just keep showing up at the gym and one day you will begin to see the difference. You will begin to think and feel differently. Instead of shoving a bag of chips in your mouth, you'll choose a piece of fruit. Instead of hating the way you look in the mirror, you'll begin to see yourself as a work in progress, not just a hopeless lump.

The same is true in the spiritual life. When you change the way you act with relation to God (and others in God), you will change the way you think and feel. When you act more loving, you will feel more loving. When you act more charitably, you will think kinder thoughts. When you act more honestly, you will become more honest.

Changes in behavior always result in changed thoughts and feelings. *Always.* The only exceptions are certain pathological conditions. But we'll leave that for another day.

So if you want to experience more zip and zest in your spiritual life; if you want to know the living God in a way that manifests his love and power in your life; if you want to live the life God created you to live; if you want to love your neighbor as the Lord wants you to — then make a change in the way you behave. I guarantee you'll be astonished at the results.

SUMMARY If you want to change, then begin with behavior. You will see results right away. You don't have to wait a lifetime to see the effects.

Appendix:
Behaviorism – Take What You Want and Leave the Rest

This appendix is written as a response to many spiritual writers and theologians who have reacted so negatively even to the thought that possibly behaviorism might have something useful to say about Christian spirituality. It is an invitation to "give us a chance."

It is also written for the various practitioners of psychology who left religion behind some years ago, some in hopes of finding something more satisfying.

The point here is that religion and psychology can be friends and can help each other . . . on our common journey to see our Father face to face.

There is much in this area of behavioral shaping that is useful. And much that is not. There is much that strays from science into the realm of ideology. Despite these aberrations, there are some principles of behavior that are proven to be very useful and that you can apply in your own spiritual lives with great success.

It's not hard at all to leave behind so much silliness of extreme behaviorists. I want to help you find the stuff that is useful and worth taking. You can leave the rest behind.

Let's use a simple comparison. There is much in the area of religion and spirituality that is helpful to people. But there is also much that strays into the area of magic and superstition and other harmful ideologies. As much as that is true, it does not deny the value of sound healthy religious and spiritual practices. It is not hard at all to leave behind most of the rantings of spiritual extremists. The goal in this area is also to help people find the stuff that is useful, beautiful, good, and true.

It's pretty understandable how behaviorism got such a bad name among Christians right from the start. There are many reasons. Here are some of them.

1. Psychology desperately wanted to be treated like a "real science."

Psychology wanted to take its place next to physics, chemistry, biology, and mathematics. It needed to be "hard-headed" and "coldly objective" . . . with its own scientific method and with its own canons of evidence. If your goal is to gain respect as a "real scientist," then you are going to have to put on a white coat, work in a laboratory, and do something very radical, namely, you had better try to separate yourself from the realm of religion.

B. F. Skinner did a terrific job of this. He insisted that the determinants of behavior are not inside the organism. They are outside the organism. This was not simply a methodological behaviorism, it was a philosophical behaviorism. He was sure there was nothing inside the organism worthwhile to study or to be learned from. Determinants of behavior are to be found outside the organism, not inside the organism. An individual's identity is, in Skinner's view, determined by that person's reinforcement history. Nothing more. Nothing less.

Today's advances in neurophysiology make this philosophical behaviorism less than a tenable position. But in Skinner's day, he knew little about neurophysiology.

Skinner would say that adaptive behavior, designed to meet and respond to the demands of the external world, is what life is all about. Life is not about freedom and dignity. Skinner wanted us to get beyond these. A person is best understood in terms of the environmental contingencies in that individual's history.

2. Behaviorism began with animal experiments.

On TV's *Jeopardy*, everybody gets right the question about who experimented with dogs. It was Ivan Pavlov who won the Nobel Prize for physiology in 1904. He studied digestive reflexes in dogs.

Pavlov is known for his work on conditioning. The ringing of a bell was associated with food being put on a dog's tongue, and after a few repetitions, the dog would salivate when the bell alone was sounded.

In the psychological literature, this is called classical or respondent or Pavlovian conditioning. It involves a reflex like dogs salivating. So a selected neurostimulus can be so associated with an unconditional stimulus that the response is transferred.

The fact that the Soviet Union doted on Pavlov and his experiments did much to give behaviorism a bad name among Christians too, who resented the assumption that "humans are nothing but dogs."

What happened in the Soviet Union was simple. The stridently antireligious Soviet system, which was atheistic and materialistic, latched onto behavioristic principles and carried them to an extreme. This is where lots of the stuff we would "leave behind" is found. It has nothing to do with discovering things that are real and useful . . . as science is supposed to do. It has more to do with imposing a pseudo-belief system and using science as a rationale for it.

In 1920 John B. Watson and Rosalie Rayner performed a behavioral study that left Christians and most humanists horrified. They intentionally created an intense fear of rats in a little boy named Albert. The researchers would make loud noises and scare Albert when he would reach for a rat. Through classical conditioning, Albert's fear of rats became associated with loud, fearful noises. The little boy then formed an irrational fear of all furry animals.

That story alone would leave a bad taste in most people's mouths. How could you do that to a little child?

Skinner devoted most of his time to rats and pigeons. "Train a rat . . . train a human" is a pretty scary prospect. As Daniel N. Robinson of Georgetown University points out in his *Intellectual History of Psychology*, what you learn from animal studies depends on what animals you study and what settings you put them in. If you study lab rats or pigeons, you get what Skinner got. The behavior of these small-brained animals in Skinner boxes at similar settings seems to reinforce the notion that the determinants of behavior are outside the individual rat or pigeon rather than inside.

If you study chimpanzees as Wolfgang Kohler did at the Anthropoid Station in Tenerife, you find "latent learning" and "transpositional learning." Here, it seems, determinants of behavior are also inside the animal.

3. Humans and animals aren't the same, no matter what early behaviorists claimed.

The existence of common behavioral traits among animals (pigeons and people) doesn't make them the same. For instance, cows and pigs have four feet, but we all recognize the difference between them. So too pigeons and people have common behavioral traits. We know the difference between them as well.

The positive thing to be learned from these common behavioral traits is that there are various behavioral strategies that are useful in therapy dealing with certain pathologies of human beings. The arrogance of early science missed the limitations of these useful factors. It is a common flaw of logic to hastily lump together things based on a few similarities.

Every shepherd has known for centuries that animals can be trained through reinforcement. And shepherds did not have to abandon their religious convictions in the process. After all, it was to poor shepherds that angels appeared to announce our Lord's birth! So if you adopt behavioral principles, you do not have to do so at the expense of your beliefs. You do not have to become atheistic or deterministic. A good shepherd knows the basic principles of behavior and he doesn't become a behavioral atheist. A mom knows how to potty-train her child and that doesn't make her a behavioral atheist.

4. Many early behavioral scientists were guilty of extremism.

These scientists enjoyed being treated as a threat to religion. They thought it was great. It gave them notoriety and status. And they loved to dispossess students of their religious convictions, telling them, "When you become a true scientist, you don't need that mishmash of faith."

That was very heady stuff to the young students of psychology, whose professors wore lab coats. Gullible college freshmen today are still ready to believe a variety of scholarly looking professors with a good sales pitch. And many a graduate student is eager to shed the religious faith of his childhood in order to secure the approval of his academic mentor. Talk about reinforcement!

There is an old adage that goes something like this. With the coming of Sigmund Freud, psychology lost its soul. And with the coming of Skinner, it lost its mind.

Remember the old joke about Ivan Pavlov whose dogs trained him so well that whenever they salivated, he would ring a bell and feed them?

And then there's the story about B. F. Skinner, who, it seems, enjoyed pacing on the platform while lecturing. One semester the students conspired together. Whenever Skinner came close to the edge, they would evidence great interest and write furiously in their notebooks. Within a week, they say, Skinner fell off the platform.

Fewer and fewer people today embrace the mono-explanatory views of philosophical behaviorism. But more and more people are coming to appreciate the beneficial application of behavioral principles in therapy. My intent is to help folks understand how behavioral principles apply in the spiritual life as well.

We have neither time nor space to talk about the huge advances that have been made in studies of the physiology of the brain and the new insights that are being gained. Roger W. Sperry received a Nobel Prize for his research on the functional differences between the two hemispheres of the human cortex. He proposes that behavior is not just neurologically determined, but also subjectively driven. And he speaks about this as "the cognitive revolution."

Studies are also being done on the heart's electrical signals that may shape the way the brain thinks about certain kinds of events. Some scientists are using insights from the physiology of the heart (different from using the mind or muscles as is done in traditional yoga or meditation or traditional psycho-therapy), and these seem promising or at least worth a try as a faster way to disengage certain destructive emotional habits.

5. The language of behaviorism is cold and technical.

It is the language of animal experiments . . . the language of control. The notion popularized by Skinner pictured behaviorism as creating generations of humans acting as robots. That's why behavioral therapy in its initial forms was roundly criticized as unthinking, unfeeling, unreligious, and robotic. At the root of this language of control was the deterministic assumption that all appeals to inner-psychological phenomena (as explanations of human behavior) are inferential. They are not genuinely explanatory. And thus they can be safely ignored as nonexistent. Human behavior, in this scheme, is explained by environmental factors outside the human being rather than by reference to some "homunculus" inside. In other words, it is all determined. Forget about free will. It is said that B. F. Skinner wrote *Beyond Freedom and Dignity* in response to C. S. Lewis's *The Abolition of Man*.

Some of us were first introduced to behaviorism by reading two books in high school. The first was Skinner's *1984* and the other was George Orwell's *Animal Farm*. Both of them captured the imagination of the American people during the Korean War when Communist brainwashing was being used on American POW's. It fit the ideology of a dictator to say: "There is no morality . . . just behavior."

Behavioral Principles Are Not Ideological Belief Systems

Let's not throw the baby out with the bathwater. Principles of behavior exist apart from any ideological belief systems of behaviorists. So we can learn from principles of behavior and forget about the philosophical assumptions of atheism and determinism.

Principles of Behavior

Principles of behavior do exist. We should become aware of them. One does not have to abandon one's religious beliefs to understand these principles of behavior and apply them. In fact, they exist quite harmoniously to further explain the goodness of a world created by God.

Let us take a look at a few of them.

1. The relationship between reinforcement and behavior.

If an action meets with success, it is likely to be repeated. That's true for us human beings just as it is true for an animal that learns that by pressing on a bar it will receive a pellet of food . . . not just once but every time it presses on the bar. This is called continuous reinforcement.

I find it very interesting too that sometimes you have to do something two or three times to get a positive consequence. And when you learn how this works, you practice it faithfully. For example, Skinner developed a scheme whereby a food pellet would drop down for every second tap on the bar (or peck if it was a pigeon). Given this state of affairs, the pigeon would go over to the bar and immediately tap twice instead of once. This is called partial reinforcement, that is to say, not every response gets the reward.

If a pigeon was rewarded with a food pellet for every fifth peck on the bar, behaviorists would say that pigeon was on a "fixed ratio of 5" schedule of reinforcement . . . five pecks on the bar and there is an immediate reward. One legendary pigeon was trained to peck so hard and so fast on the "fixed ratio of 38" schedule of reinforcement that his bill became hot, causing the lever to smoke.

We humans respond in the same way as pigeons. If something "good" happens when we behave in a certain way, we are likely to continue doing it. Many employment practices in the post-modern world are based on the relationship between reinforcement and behavior.

In addition to fixed ratio schedules, the schedule of reinforcement for pigeons and rats could be more varied. These variable ratio schedules are akin to the Las Vegas slot machines: the slot machines pay off on some "variable schedule." The player does not know when the reinforcer (the jackpot) will be delivered. With some humans, this variable rate schedule maintains stable rates of behavior indefinitely. The gamblers just keep playing and playing and playing.

So you go to Las Vegas and you're playing the machines, not knowing when you will win the big one. Such partial reinforcement leads to high rates of persistent respondence. This is a principle of behavior well known and used by the lotteries across America.

2. The importance of avoidance conditioning.

Skinner performed an experiment in which he put an animal in the box and he wired the floor in such a way that a few seconds after the light went on, the animal was hit by a jolt of electricity. There was a little fence in this cage and the other side of the fence was "safe." That is to say, there was no electric shock there. If the rat jumps over the fence, he can escape the shock. It is interesting to note that it only takes one or two or three of these routines, and as the light is turned on, the animal jumps to safety and avoids the electric shock. And the animal continues to jump to safety over and over and over again. It no longer matters if the electric shock is turned on or not. The animal jumps to avoid it just as soon as a light goes on.

This type of avoidance conditioning is equally prevalent in our species. For example, your teacher so humiliated you one day when you volunteered to get up in front of the class and recite a poem that you have never ever volunteered to speak in public again.

3. The principle of cognitive dissonance.

This is nothing more than thinking one way and acting in a different way. If this goes on for a period of time, it is very likely that one will be brought into conformity with the other by changing either the thinking or the behavior.

4. The usefulness of operational definitions.

These definitions limit themselves to what is external and observable. For example, a non-operational definition of prayer would be: raising the mind and heart to God. An operational definition of prayer would be: sitting quietly in church, focusing your eyes on the tabernacle, concentrating on feeling the presence of the Lord, saying traditional or spontaneous prayers. This is very helpful in spiritual growth and development.

An operational definition of charity is: feeding the hungry, giving drink to the thirsty. A non-operational definition is: having a big heart. Sometimes it is easy to develop an operational definition. The degree to which the thing you are defining can be pointed at is the degree to which it is easy.

On the other hand, it is very difficult to give an operational definition of the rich varieties of justice: you can't point at distributive justice. Of course, you can point at the rudimentary forms of justice: "That toy belongs to your sister. You can't keep it. You need to give it back to her." This is helpful.

Other Helpful Distinctions

Here are other helpful distinctions to keep in mind.

1. The difference between accidental reinforcement and planned reinforcement.
Accidental reinforcement happens all the time:

- You wear a certain dress one day. Two people compliment you. What happens? You tend to wear it more often. That wasn't their intention, but it happens anyway.
- You wear a certain shirt and your wife says, "That doesn't look very good on you." It is just an offhand comment. But you tend to put it back in the closet and not wear it again. That wasn't her plan, but it happens anyway.
- Your child wants something and you say no. The child yells, screams, and hollers and you say no again. The child screams more and more and more until you say yes. You have just taught your child: "If at first you don't succeed, holler louder and you will succeed."
- You praise the tapioca pudding. Lo and behold, more tapioca pudding appears time and again for dessert. (You obviously don't end up with tapioca for dessert every day. So you are not like a pigeon pecking on a bar.)

This is all accidental or non-intentional reinforcement and it happens all the time.

Then there is planned reinforcement, or what Skinner calls operant conditioning. It's not Applied Behavioral Analysis, but it is still operant conditioning.

- You are potty-training your little boy. When he tells you he has to go to the bathroom, hops on the potty, and does his business, you praise him a lot.
- Your child has difficulty in reading and you've made it a goal to help her read better. You praise her when she reads out loud to you.
- You want to pray for ten minutes every day while driving to work. When you do so, you intentionally give yourself a reward.
- You have a hard time being civil to your mother-in-law and are working on this. When you succeed, you intentionally reward yourself.

2. The difference between training/behavioral learning and education.

In physics I learned the principles of thermodynamics. This is education, not training. In math I learned trigonometry. In literature I read Homer, Ovid, and Graham Greene. These are forms of education, not training. *Education* has a lot to do with insights and creativity, memorizing and logical thinking. It is "inside" us. *Training*, or behavioral learning, involves teaching skills and building relationships. These begin "outside" us. Both are important.

3. The difference between using reinforcement for some things and reinforcement for everything.

Mono-explanatory reinforcement simply refers to folks who use reinforcement to explain everything. It is the only instrument in their child-rearing repertoire. The classic example is that of John B. Watson, who suggested to parents that his own kind of "scientific behavioral psychology" could set children on the path of being whatever the parent desired – a professor of biology, an anthropologist, a dentist, etc. To say the project did not meet with success is an understatement. But it hasn't kept some parents from trying.

The most recent example is the self-esteem movement in education. This movement has neither good results nor good reinforcement. In other words, the behavior of saints and sinners cannot simply be explained by their reinforcement history. Saints are those individuals blessed with the grace of God touching their hearts and lives, to which they have responded enthusiastically. Mother Teresa is a good example.

Behaviorism Can Complement Christianity

Many of the pioneers in psychology were afraid of religion. They thought it was an enemy of science. They suffered from an undifferentiated view of religion. Many of them reduced religion down to the fundamentalist belief that truth can only be found "in the book." A few of these pioneers were clever hucksters, gaining followers by mocking established religions.

Physicians today are now saying that people who pray often get better faster . . . so science is catching up. It is no longer afraid that religious practices will destroy all science. Religion and science are not the same. They can be friends and allies. Most people have known that for centuries. And the scientists are finally catching up.

Depressed mental patients who find religion important in their lives often recover faster than patients who are less religious. People who have a "fighting spirit" when faced with cancer or other life-threatening diseases generally live longer than those who don't.

In conclusion I hope you can now understand better the title of this appendix: "Behaviorism — Take What You Want and Leave the Rest." It just seems to me that there are two extremes to be avoided:

- The first is to consider religious belief to be the same as superstition and magic and therefore to reduce all discussions of spirituality to simplistic behavioral components.
- The second is to consider time-tested behavioral principles to be out of bounds and having nothing to do with our spiritual lives. This is equivalent to saying I am so mysterious and so far above the natural world that none of these rules apply to me.

Wisdom occurs when we avoid these extremes. Religion and spirituality are not destroyed by known and applicable behavioral principles; rather, they can be enhanced.

Notes

Notes

Notes

Notes

Notes

Notes

Notes

Our Sunday Visitor. . .
Your Source for Discovering
the Riches of the Catholic Faith

Our Sunday Visitor has an extensive line of materials for young children, teens, and adults. Our books, Bibles, booklets, CD-ROMs, audios, and videos are available in bookstores worldwide. To receive a FREE full-line catalog or for more information, call **Our Sunday Visitor** at **1-800-348-2440**. Or write, **Our Sunday Visitor** / 200 Noll Plaza / Huntington, IN 46750.

- -

Please send me: ___A catalog
Please send me materials on:
___Apologetics and catechetics   ___Reference works
___Prayer books   ___Heritage and the saints
___The family   ___The parish
Name_____
Address_____Apt._____
City_____State_____Zip_____
Telephone (   ) _____
                                            A19BBABP

- -

Please send a friend: ___A catalog
Please send a friend materials on:
___Apologetics and catechetics   ___Reference works
___Prayer books   ___Heritage and the saints
___The family   ___The parish
Name_____
Address_____Apt._____
City_____State_____Zip_____
Telephone (   ) _____
                                            A19BBABP

- -

OUR
SUNDAY
VISITOR
BOOKS

Our Sunday Visitor
200 Noll Plaza
Huntington, IN 46750
Toll free: 1-800-348-2440
E-mail: osvbooks@osv.com
Website: www.osv.com